Paul T. Hellyer,

a native of Waterford, Ontario, has been involved in federal politics in Canada since his first election to Parliament in 1949, after graduation from the University of Toronto. He has also found time to become a very successful businessman, associated with construction and real estate firms in Toronto.

A renegade from the Trudeau Cabinet and the Founding Chairman of *Action Canada*, Paul Hellyer is one of Canada's most dynamic and controversial political figures. He was the Opposition defence critic during the Diefenbaker regime. In 1963, Prime Minister Lester Pearson appointed him Minister of National Defence. He was responsible for amalgamating the Canadian Army, Navy and Air Force into a single service—The Canadian Armed Forces. One of the chief contenders in the Liberal leadership race of 1968, won by Pierre Trudeau, he became Minister of Transport and Minister in Charge of Housing. During his Cabinet career a number of publicly-owned corporations have reported to him or through him to Parliament, including The Canadian National Railway, Air Canada, The Canadian Overseas Telecommunications Corporation, and Central Mortgage and Housing Corporation. He resigned his Cabinet post in 1969 to protest what he viewed as the government's unwillingness to give positive leadership in the federal aspects of housing and urban development.

In 1971, he resigned from the Liberal Caucus to sit as an Independent Liberal. A growing realization that effective action was impossible within the existing political structure led to the founding of *Action Canada* in May, 1971. Drawing support from all parts of the political spectrum, *Action Canada* proposes positive policies to provide full employment and stable prices as the financial and social basis necessary for concentration on the "quality of life" issues.

Mr. Hellyer is married to the former Ellen Jean Ralph. They have three children, Mary Elizabeth, Peter and David.

Agenda: A Plan for Action underscores the urgency to cut through the words, the clichés and the myths, if we are to solve the economic problems that face us today. The book expresses, in layman's terms, Mr. Hellyer's unequivocal rejection of socialism and his conviction that any free, open society can be operated with full employment and zero inflation within the private capital system. Mr. Hellyer warns that it is economic mismanagement and incompetence that causes unemployment, inflation and inequitable (as opposed to equal) distribution of income.

The number one problem in Canada and the United States today is "cost-push" inflation, where increases in costs have exceeded increases in productivity. This condition, argues Mr. Hellyer, is a product of the structure of the modern private capital economy. The structure is characterized by a split between an oligopolistic sector of huge unions and corporations and a competitive sector of unorganized workers and small businesses. The power of the oligopolistic sector cannot be effectively confronted by classic economic policy. New methods are needed and Mr. Hellyer's major policy recommendation is that mandatory wage and price controls are necessary to the regulation of the non-competitive part of the economy. Mr. Hellyer is not suggesting that government set individual wages or prices, but that it must enforce guidelines based on the average annual increase in physical output in real terms.

Mr. Hellyer's liberalism is dynamic and humane:

> "I believe that rational change can best take place in a decentralized society where man, not the State, is supreme. Rational change will permit us to keep our basic freedoms, and to add those new ones necessary to enhance our quality of life. Full employment and stable prices will give us the maximum range of choice with which to assert equality of opportunity and justice for all. This is the liberalism I espouse. It is not a liberalism of the left or of the right but, I believe, a rational and, above all, humane liberalism."

AGENDA

a Plan for ACTION

by

Paul T. Hellyer

PRENTICE HALL OF CANADA LTD.

Scarborough, Ontario

p
h

PRENTICE-HALL, INC., ENGLEWOOD CLIFFS, NEW JERSEY
PRENTICE-HALL OF AUSTRALIA, PTY., LTD., SYDNEY
PRENTICE-HALL OF INDIA PVT., LTD., NEW DELHI
PRENTICE-HALL INTERNATIONAL, INC., LONDON
PRENTICE-HALL OF JAPAN, INC., TOKYO

HD
82
.H455
1971

Library of Congress Catalog Card No. 70-173594
ISBN   0-13-018572-8

PRINTED IN CANADA   1 2 3 4 5   75 74 73 72 71

Table of Contents

Preface

"Young man, you are too young to remember the great depression." That summary dismissal, by one of my senior parliamentary colleagues, of my "sermon" on monetary and fiscal mismanagement was the reaction that infuriated me most. Actually, I do remember the depression years very well. It is true that I suffered no personal hardship. I was young and my family did not miss a square meal though that was due more to the embarrassment than to the benevolence of our creditor, the bank. The size of our loan was too large in relationship to our realizable assets; consequently, we were kept in the farming business until the postwar years and the return of prosperity.

My experience of the depression thus was not one of personal suffering. But I had eyes and ears. The amount of human misery and suffering that I saw all around me burned an indelible impression in my mind. The depression seemed to be the ultimate in human stupidity. Something was desperately wrong. The Canadian banking system, which prided itself on the fact that no Canadian bank had defaulted during the 1930's, neglected to say that this record was only made possible by putting thousands of small businesses into bankruptcy and hundreds of thousands of Canadian workers into the breadlines. The politicians, for the most part, were no more enlightened and were accessories to these crimes against their own people committed in the name of financial orthodoxy.

Many young people, like myself, found the whole episode incredible. Thousands upon thousands of people who had been working and planning their lives were suddenly faced with enormous incomprehensible hardships. Carpenters and plumbers stood in lines waiting for the work that wasn't there. Their wives and children lived in poor, often desperately poor, housing. They lacked food. At the same time, farmers were pouring milk into the fields and down sewers. Baby pigs were killed and then buried for lack of markets. People without food and farmers without markets! People without housing and carpenters without jobs! The order of economic society had collapsed.

The physical capability was there. In most cases, it was just as great as it had been in 1929. But the system of production and distribution had broken down in a most disastrous way. Of course then, as now, there were false comforters of fear and defenders of stupidity. Economic theologians tried to rationalize the situation as just one of a series of inevitable cycles, a period of readjustment. Some of the "other" theologians drew God into the mess. The prairie drought was compared to the seven lean years suffered in the days of Abraham. There were dissenters, but they were labelled as heretics or cranks.

Why didn't revolution sweep one country after another during the depression? I do not know. Certainly there were many converts to communism, especially among the intellectuals. One wonders why there were not more. I would not care to guess the reasons why so many put up with so much for so long, but the fact is they did—and frequently quite cheerfully. But why, why, did it have to happen?

It was with this question fresh in my mind that I entered college after two unproductive years in the Armed Forces. I took an introductory course in political economy because, by then, I wanted to know what made the world tick. Instead, I discovered what made the professors talk. At first I thought it was a "put on." I soon realized that I was mistaken and that all the old orthodoxy was being intoned in deadly serious fashion. I was shattered. It was then that "the heresies" began to crystallize in my mind.

To be sure, my worst fears of that period have not material-ized, due partly to another tragedy of war, the Korean war, which prevented a possible recession from developing in the early 1950's. Subsequently, the mysteries of "growth" have become much better understood and in perspective we have come a long way in the last twenty years.

This prompts some to speak of our having solved the "economic problem." In fact, this is far from the truth. We face a new dilemma today, the dilemma of unemployment and inflation. How do you fight one without encouraging the other? Some western countries, notably Canada and the United States, have high unemployment and unacceptable inflation at the same time. Others, such as Japan, Sweden and Germany, have little if any unemployment but relatively high inflation.

There also remains a problem of income distribution, which varies in degree from country to country but which, along with other issues related both to equity and the quality of life, causes considerable dissatisfaction. The dissatisfaction, in turn, is the spawning and feeding ground for a new wave of radicalism—more widespread and intense than anything we have known in the last thirty years.

In view of these and other problems and the suffering and unrest they cause, it is essential that we re-examine our economic situation. In doing so we face an elementary choice. On the one hand, we may abandon hope for our system and decide to scrap it. This presupposes alternatives. On the other hand, we may decide that what is wrong is correctable.

Although I think such a choice is fundamental and pre-cedes any policy, it will be obvious where I stand. A basic purpose of this book is to show unequivocally why I reject the only major alternative to our economic system. I mean Socialism or State Capital. My basic objection is perfectly simple: it does not work. Furthermore, the obsessive attempt to make it work leads to abuses that are far more serious than the problems we now face. In the words of the young, contemporary socialism is part of the problem, not part of the solution.

Having rejected socialism, the book turns to its essential task, which is economic reform within the context of our private capital system. More specifically, I have attempted to prove that it is possible to operate a free open society with full employment and zero inflation. To accomplish this requires first of all a basic intellectual adjustment. We must admit that our economies have changed from the days of "perfect" competition. Our economies are now split: while one part continues to be competitive and to be governed by market forces, another part, composed of monopolies and oligopolies, enjoys enormous power. It is that power which renders ineffective the traditional tools of economic management. It is that power which must be confronted.

In response to this basic fact, the major policy recommendation of the book is that mandatory wage and price controls are necessary to the regulation of the non-competitive part of our economies. These controls would extend to those large corporations and unions that have such decisive influence on the overall economy. Both the rationale and the mechanics of these proposals will be discussed in considerable detail.

The basic obstacle to this recommendation is outmoded ideas. We will have to unlearn many of the economic myths that we were taught in school or that have been passed on from one generation to another. Without attempting a catalogue, some of the more obvious ones are: a little inflation is a good thing; inflation is necessary to maintain full employment; people have to be retired earlier to provide jobs for the young; working wives take jobs away from male heads of household who need employment; capitalism can only prosper during war or with rumours of war; capital exploits (gets greater rewards than) labour; capitalism would collapse if there were a real peace; gold is necessary to promote international trade; business cycles are inevitable; inflation is inevitable; recessions and depressions are natural adjustments; and it is necessary to have a shelved public works program ready to fill the gap when the cycle turns down and unemployment rises. These are all myths based on misinterpretations of economic history. They are all subject to challenge and should be challenged.

It is not the system that is at fault, but the management of the system. That is my thesis. Whereas some would say that the system is fundamentally unworkable and would be prepared to reject it, I suggest that the real problem has been the failure of our society to adapt its institutions quickly enough to cope with the consequences of changing technology. If we had done so, the problems of recessions and depressions would never have occurred in the first place. Our failure to react quickly enough, however, is a natural manifestation of man's basically conservative makeup and the root cause of most of the periodic misery and hardship associated with economic development since the Industrial Revolution. Ideas, however, can change.

The problems that are regarded as traditional in the open system are soluble. I am not naive enough to suggest that solutions are easy or automatic. Even when theoretically simple, a solution must overcome the unspeakable rigidity of men's minds. But this is possible, with persistence. It can be done. That fresh approaches are necessary is self-evident. That the stakes are high is also obvious. How high, one can only speculate. Failure to improve our performance both in real terms and in the method of presentation could result in escalating chaos and a subsequent loss of freedom which, at the moment, is in the "it can't happen here" drawer of consciousness. The "improved system" that I wish to discuss will provide the mechanics and a range of choice far superior to any existing or likely alternative. A timely introduction may avoid unnecessary recrimination and possible violence. It is a golden opportunity to lead the way.

Let me make one final prefatory comment. I have striven to make this book as clear and straightforward as possible. Some may feel that I spend too much time on fundamentals and in discussing the "grand alternatives." But I have my reasons for that and ask for the reader's patience. I believe that fundamentals are . . . well, fundamental.

P.T.H.

Acknowledgments

I wish to express my sincere appreciation to a number of people who helped me in my work: to my family for giving up the use of the dining room table for so many weeks; to the scores of economists, bankers, labour-leaders and businessmen who gave so freely of their time; to the girls who typed the manuscript; to Dr. Harvey Schwartz of York University for a number of very useful and helpful suggestions; to Mrs. Clare McKeon for sensitive and gentle editing; and especially to Bob Miller for his painstaking research and thoughtful collaboration. Without him, the text would never have been completed.

Finally, a special word of gratitude to the Canadian taxpayers for providing more than twenty years of the best postgraduate training any man could ask for.

AGENDA

a Plan for Action

PART ONE

A Brief Review

Chapter 1

The Industrial Revolution
and the
Money Famine

For generations, most human energy was directed toward the simple pursuits of ensuring an adequate food supply. As this became relatively easier a wide range of crafts developed and skilled artisans, though small in numbers, built the cities, the artifacts and the tools required for their civilizations. It was only with the Industrial Revolution, however, and the wholesale harnessing of inanimate energy that the profound developments and accelerating rate of change of the nineteenth and twentieth centuries became possible.

The evolution of large parts of the world from primarily agrarian pursuits to primarily industrial pursuits has been as rocky as it has been interesting and full of promise. In Canada, for example, a little over one hundred years ago the great majority of the population was engaged in agriculture. Today, less than 10 per cent and soon about 5 per cent of the working population will be able to produce all the food required domestically and large quantities for export as well. This phenomenon – and it really is phenomenal – is a direct result of the application of technology to agriculture.

The other aspect of this evolution is industrial growth and the ability of industry to provide gainful employment for the large numbers of displaced agricultural workers as well as new entrants to the labour force. These processes, along with their inevitable conflicts, have been well recorded and it is not my intention to repeat the story. It is necessary, however, to examine one or two aspects in order to place in context both the problems that are historically associated with capitalism and the suggestions to be discussed later.

The process of economic development, which has so profoundly changed our way of life, is composed of a number of related factors. These include growth in the quantity and quality of capital, expansion of knowledge, improvement in the skills of labour and changes in the organization of work. Although it is impossible to measure the exact contribution made by each factor, it is clear that capital, its availability and quality, is of fundamental importance.

What is capital? Perhaps I can best begin to answer that with a homey example. If a farmer cuts down ten trees, burns seven for fuel and makes planks of the remaining three, the seven are "consumption" and the three are "savings." If he then invests his time and planks in the building of a wagon he has created a capital good. The wagon could be used to clear his fields or to move produce more efficiently than if the farmer were confined to using his hands and shoulders. And the point is, quite simply, more food for the farmer and for others.

As this example illustrates, capital is a material enlargement of man's physical and mental capacity. It is used with labour and natural resources to produce goods and services. Unlike labour and natural resources, capital is not found naturally but is generated through a process of invention, savings and investment. Savings means "putting something aside." Investment means employing all or part of savings in the creation of capital goods. These, in turn, are not ends in themselves but are valuable, for they contribute to economic development and mean a better standard of living in the future.

This elementary value of capital means that men will pay a price (rent) for it. If our fictitious farmer had no need for his wagon for a few weeks he would be faced with an economic choice. A neighbour might wish to borrow the wagon for a few days to clear a field or several neighbours might wish to borrow the wagon at the same time. The farmer-owner then has the choice of lending the wagon to one of his neighbours on the basis of friendship or personal obligation or of renting it on the strictly economic basis of ability to pay. Remembering the tremendous effort he put into building the wagon and the probability that an arbitrary choice on his part would alienate the affection of all his neighbours other than the chosen one, the farmer will, in the majority of cases, make his choice by renting the wagon (capital) to the highest bidder.

When we think of capital today, of course, we usually think of something much more sophisticated, such as huge factories with giant machines. But these, in reality, are just large agglomerations of capital goods, vast quantities of planks (wood or steel), shingles, bricks and machines. The principles involved in their use are exactly the same. It is true, however, that the size of modern capital formation creates special institutional problems. We will return to this subject later.

There are two points I would like to make now. First, all industrialized countries are capitalist. It was capital accumulation that made industrialization possible in the first place. In a sense, we confuse the issues when we refer to some industrialized countries as capitalist and others as socialist or communist, because these terms refer only to the forms of government and to the methods of administering the capital, which itself is ubiquitous. For my purposes, then, I will refer to countries as state capital countries if the majority of the capital assets are held by the state and administered on behalf of the state. Countries where the majority of the capital assets are held privately and administered by privately-owned corporations, will be referred to as private capital countries. I deliberately use "majority of capital assets" in the definitions because few if any economic systems are exclusively public or private. Canada, for example, is essentially a private capital economy, but with a significant number of public corporations. Poland is largely a state capital system but with some allowance for the private ownership of assets such as small farms.

Second, the benefits derived from the use of capital are

very great. The wealthiest countries in the world, or at least those with the highest average incomes, are those with the greatest capital accumulations per person. Economic growth and, subsequently, income depend to a considerable extent on capital. There is, consequently, a worldwide shortage of capital and worldwide competition for the opportunity to use available resources. This competition, primarily though not exclusively in the private capital world, affects the price that people are willing to pay for the use of capital and imposes restraints on any country because a country cannot adopt policies that make capital investment unattractive and, at the same time, expect to compete for large capital investments from abroad.

It was the very large contribution capital goods make to production that Marx did not understand or, possibly, refused to recognize. Reading Marx, one cannot escape the conclusion that he was primarily a theologian, in the sense that he spent tremendous energy constructing abstractions which gain absolute credibility by the simple device of ignoring economic realities. In this sense, he did not differ from the classical economists who had influenced him so greatly.

Marx argued that, in the production of commodities, only labour produced a surplus. Capital goods, which Marx called constant capital, contributed only the value of the labour embodied in their production. By so arguing, he ignored the facts. He attributed the extra output made possible by the use of capital goods (compared with the direct application of labour to natural resources), to labour alone and called it surplus value. But this surplus value is nothing more than "rent" for the use of capital. It is a payment for the extra output that the use of capital makes possible. It takes the form of interest on borrowed savings or of profit to the risk capital provided by the owners of business.

Surplus value, then, is nothing more than "rent" for capital. In modern parlance, it is called profit. Perhaps that is a pity, because profit has become a dirty word with many well-meaning reformers. Most of them would not deny a reasonable "rent" for capital, especially if the capital were their own. Those who mouth the old cliché "produce for need, not for profit" are merely demonstrating an ignorance of economic processes. It is one of life's sadder truths that good intentions do not, by themselves, make good economics.

The questions of what to produce and the rate of return on capital involve many considerations of priority. No matter what is produced, however, and whether it is needed or not, the rate of return on capital must be sufficient to persuade someone to invest. In view of the world shortage, it is interesting to note that the return on capital in recent years has been relatively modest, on average, in real terms.

Although it was capital and its owners, "the capitalists," who became the focus of Marx's fury, it was the degradation of the working classes and the periodic economic crises that influenced him profoundly and provided the driving motive for his work. Like Rodbertus before him, and hundreds of other economists since, Marx thought that "the capitalist continually tended to produce more than the market for his goods would absorb. Products would not ordinarily be 'cleared' as in a natural or barter economy."[1] In *Ideas of the Great Economists*, George Soule goes on to say: "This was the cause of the frequently recurring periods in which a surplus of goods in the hands of the capitalist was accompanied by unemployment and want on the part of the workers. Though Marx's theory of depression was a crude and incomplete one, he deserves credit as one of the first economic theorists to emphasize an obviously critical defect in the operation of a capitalist order."

The fact remains that having recognized the obvious defect, Marx did not recognize the less obvious reason for it. He failed to see the fly in the ointment.

Gold was the Fly in the Ointment

Gold had been used as money for centuries. In addition to its intrinsic value for jewelry, adornments, etc., gold had a certain mystic quality. It is worth noting that when the three Wise Men attended the baby Jesus, "They presented unto him gifts: gold and frankincense and myrrh".[2] Obviously it headed the list of things esteemed for presentation as gifts on important occasions. The reason for this high value, no doubt, was its relative scarcity.

It is because of its relative scarcity, however, that gold was completely inappropriate as a monetary standard after the Industrial Revolution began. Capital goods married to specialized labour and technology resulted in an enormous increase in output. It became possible to increase the manufacture of "things" at a much faster rate than the supply of gold. The attempt to relate the one to the other in some rigid and basically inflexible manner created incalculable havoc with the evolving system. The use of gold or in some cases its pale sister, silver, as a monetary standard was fundamental to the recurring crises that were so deeply deplored but so poorly understood. A measurement of this misunderstanding was the fact that succeeding generations of scholars, including Marx, accepted the periodic cycles of apparent overproduction followed by depression and underutilization of resources as an inherent and incurable fault in what they referred to as the "capitalistic" system. This mistaken assumption led to error throughout their economic analyses.

In attempting to understand what went wrong, it is necessary to observe that the barter system had long since broken down. The use of precious metals (coins) in exchange had largely been supplanted first by the use of bank notes and later by the introduction of cheques as well. But the total money supply including bank notes and cheques was related not to the output of goods and services but to the level of reserves (gold and/or silver). It is true that the ratio of bank notes and deposits outstanding to reserves was changed many times to meet changing circumstances. But the change in the total money supply was not systematic. It was not directly related to the productive potential of the economy. It was rather haphazard and more likely to be related to the supply of gold than to the needs of the marketplace.

The search for clues to the solution of an obvious problem may have been hindered by observations of some of the early economists such as Jean Baptiste Say who claimed that since the production of any article creates an equivalent demand for some other article, total supply must equal total demand and, consequently, there can be no such thing as general over-production. In theory, all that is required is one gigantic market where the prices of all goods and services could be adjusted in order to "clear" the market, making way for the production of additional products and the provision of further services. But no such "perfect" market exists, certainly not on the scale required. Consequently, Say's hypothesis did not explain what it was supposed to explain. It neglected to take into account the monetary mechanics of exchange.

The mixture of specialized labour, capital goods and technology made it possible to increase the productive potential of a rapidly industrializing country by several percentage points a year. If the money supply available to purchase the goods and services remained static, or almost static, as was often the case when gold or silver standards were in vogue, all prices would have to go down an equal number of percentage points, on average, in order to clear the market. Presumably, annual wage rates must also decline in money terms, though not in real terms. However, no economic system is that flexible.

The prices of some goods and services, postage, for example, are usually set by statute. They are rigid by definition. But beyond that it is quite unnatural to expect all wages and prices to be adjusted downward more or less continuously as would be required in an expanding economy with a fixed money supply. The psychological problems are formidable. Put yourself in the hypothetical position of an employer hiring someone at an annual rate of say $5,000 and adding, as if by way of encouragement, "If all goes well you can expect a reduction in your salary of about 3% annually." It is an unnatural proposition. It is true that during the nineteenth century, in particular, wage reductions were not a rare occurrence. But these, too, were unsystematic.

Another explanation of recurring business cycles has been the wide fluctuations in the level of investment. Although, in the context of the way our economies were operated, this was a significant factor, its importance has been exaggerated. There is no reason, theoretically, why an economy should not be able to adjust rapidly to changing priorities between capital and consumer goods. No matter what the priority adequate aggregate demand is essential to maximum performance. This did not always occur in the real world, and hence the cycles. The myths of money were strangling the Industrial Revolution. Technology had changed and was changing at an ever increasing pace but the consequential institutional changes lagged hopelessly behind. This inability to react quickly to changing technology seems to be a basic law of human nature.

It is a pity, perhaps, that paper currency was called money in the first place. If it had been called "chits" or anything else rather than money, its role in the scheme of things might have been better understood. A "chit" for labour performed. A "chit" for rental of capital goods. "Chits," in either case representing a claim on goods and services for current consumption or, if current consumption was not desired, a claim on existing or new capital goods. Of course, the "chits" could have been hoarded as a matter of personal choice but this would have been self-defeating when compared with the two alternatives.

"Chits" are not commodities in the sense that bread and cheese and gold are commodities. "Chits" have no intrinsic value. They are only a symbol or standard of value which in our modern economy must refer to the amount of goods and services they will claim, not to the amount of gold found in California, or the Klondike, or South Africa, or any other place.

So we got off to a bad start by employing gold, a commodity valuable in its own right and with a very inelastic supply, as our monetary standard. Had we used a more flexible reserve than gold or silver, we would have been in less trouble. In Canada, for instance, we have used wampum,[3] beaver skins and playing cards as money at one time or another. Any of these have what the economists would call an elastic supply. This is particularly true of wampum and playing cards, although in the case of beaver skins, it might be a bit difficult to find sufficient poplar trees to support a vastly increased beaver population. Also, with beaver skins you would run the risk that some popular figure would start a beaver coat fad that would reduce dramatically the supply of skins available for Fort Knox and thus bring on a major recession and possible economic collapse.

Wampum, provided they were not mistaken for "love beads," would be a more reliable standard. Production would have to be strictly controlled, obviously, to prevent a general inflation. But subject to the proper bureaucratic safeguards, wampum would be a tremendous improvement on gold. Perhaps if one of the early managing directors of a central bank had been a woman, the use of beads on a regulated basis might have been seriously considered. Regretfully this was never the case. These august posts have been held, for the most part, by High Priests of financial orthodoxy.

Playing cards I have rejected out of hand as a monetary standard. First, playing cards are associated with gambling and I think there has already been far too much gambling involved in monetary matters. Secondly, some religious denominations, including the one in which I was raised, still regard playing cards as the work of the devil. In deference to them, and because our idolatry of gold has already brought untold hardships on millions of innocent people, playing cards are out.

We have made great progress in monetary matters in the last thirty years and, although much remains to be done, this particular range of problems is now better understood and, consequently, more intelligently managed. Notwithstanding the unfortunate consequences that flowed from confusing paper money "chits" with gold and silver reserves, we seem to have passed the point of no return and, consequently, need not change the name at this late date. But we should know what we are talking about and remember that money is "chits" for labour provided, rental for capital goods, and so on. When we want to talk about gold, silver or playing cards, we can call them by their proper names.

Notes

1. From *Ideas of the Great Economists* by George Soule. Copyright © 1952 by George Soule. All rights reserved. Reprinted by permission of the Viking Press, Inc.
2. Matthew 2:2.
3. A form of beads used by some North American Indians.

Chapter **2**

The Keynesian Revolution

The extent of governmental intervention in economic affairs during the twentieth century has accelerated rapidly. This first occurred during World War I when the disruption in normal economic relationships and requirements was so great that direct intervention, on a scale previously considered unthinkable, was essential. Later, during World War II, planning and regulation in economic matters was considered essential from the outset and fundamental to the mobilization of maximum resources without creating runaway inflation.

It was the intervening years, particularly those of the Great Depression, which again proved that "it is difficult to teach an old dog new tricks." The economic theology of youth and college days was the economic theology of old age and the grave. Most of the reigning bankers and bureaucrats had been trained in the classical school and, consequently, they failed to understand the consequences of the technological revolution that had been taking place around them. When logic failed, divine sanction was called upon to rationalize misery and suffering.

So strong were the traditional beliefs that an attempt was made to put most industrialized nations back on the gold standard in the mid-1920's. Even Winston Churchill was captive of orthodoxy. As Chancellor of the Exchequer, he was largely responsible for England's return to the gold standard at the old parity. In his Budget speech of April 28, 1925, he declared that

A return to the gold standard has long been a settled and declared policy of this country. Every Expert Conference since the war . . . has urged in principle the return to the gold standard. No responsible authority has advocated any other policy.[1]

Churchill stressed the importance of the simultaneous action of Holland, the Dutch East Indies, Australia and New Zealand, and the proposed return of South Africa, as well as the previous adoption of the gold standard by the other countries. The advantages of this common international action were pictured in his metaphor:

That standard [the gold standard] may of course vary in itself from time to time, but the position of all countries related to it will vary together like ships in a harbour whose gangways are joined and who rise and fall together with the tide.

Churchill based his case primarily on the *Report of the Committee on the Currency and Bank of England Note Issues*. The arguments of the Committee were brief and clear as far as they went, although they were described as *jejeune* by J. M. Keynes. They never explored the general desirability of a gold standard from the point of view of the interests of the different social classes affected by its operation. The general advantages of a gold standard were not stated by the report, but were taken for granted as self-evident.

In fact, the return of the gold standard only intensified the problem of industrial expansion in England and complicated the international exchange aspects of trade development. Furthermore, Churchill's metaphor was more intuitive than he guessed. With the ebb tide of liquidity at the outset of the great depression, the "ships in the harbour" sank into the mud and lay there, immobile, until 1939 when the rising tide of mobilization expenditure raised the rusty hulls.

It is not surprising that many ordinary people, intellectually repelled by what they saw, tried to find a path for penetrating the monetary jungle. It was obvious to them, or so they thought, that there was a shortage of purchasing power to buy all the goods and services available. In economic terms, it was a shortage of "aggregate demand." Unfortunately, most of the original thinking in this field was done by non-economists who, because they were not professionally trained, generally, were regarded as "cranks." Many of their solutions were "half-baked" but they contained a germ of truth that was long unrecognized by the great majority of professional economists who had, for the most part, gone to the same schools and who held to the same general economic theology.

One of the protestants was a British engineer, Major C. H. Douglas. Major Douglas believed that the pattern of income and expenditure flows in a capitalistic economy led inevitably to a shortage of purchasing power in the hands of consumers.

In other words, for any given period, the purchasing power available for buying current output was insufficient to acquire that output at prices sufficiently high to cover its total costs of production. Thus, if "overproduction" were to be avoided, a continuous injection of new purchasing power was required.

To explain his position, Major Douglas employed his celebrated "A+B" theorem, in which he divided all costs of production into two categories. The "A" costs included all payments that producers ("factories") made to individuals, such as wages, salaries and dividends, the "B" costs all payments made to organizations for such things as raw materials, machinery, maintenance of plant, bank charges, etc. Thus for any period, the total costs of production were represented by A+B, but the amount of money available to purchase the output of the period was only A, because B costs were largely in the nature of business "reserves", mere book-keeping items which, while included in total costs of production, did not represent income distributed...[2]

The A+B theorem did not add up mathematically and was quickly demolished by the experts. In their zeal to discredit the theory, however, they failed to recognize the object of the exercise: that there was, in fact, an almost chronic shortage of purchasing power. Major Douglas may not have understood the reason for it, but at least he recognized the obvious. His formula did not make sense, but the objective did. He did not have the answer, but in drawing attention to the problem, he added fuel to the fires of controversy that have persisted to this day. His followers came almost exclusively from the ranks of the laymen because his pedigree was not acceptable in academic circles. There, orthodoxy prevailed.

There were, of course, some exceptions:

Irving Fisher (1867-1947), professor of economics at Yale in the early twentieth century, concentrated on monetary problems with the hope of stabilizing prices and so moderating both booms and depressions. He, and those who agreed with him, reasoned as follows. Rising prices are the result of too much money; falling prices of too little. Everybody agrees that extreme inflation, when prices rise so high that money becomes virtually worthless, and panics, when loans become temporarily unobtainable, should be prevented. But it is important also to avoid more moderate fluctuations of the general price level, since rising prices encourage everybody to buy in the hope of speculative profits and falling prices lead everybody to sell, or refrain from buying. These alternate waves of buying and selling intensify the irregularity of business activity and employment.

What is "too much" or "too little" money? The practical test was, Fisher thought, what happened to prices; rising prices should lead to restriction of the money supply, falling prices to its expansion. Therefore the "stable-money" advocates spent much laborious study on statistical measures of prices, to obtain what they could regard as a representative index of price tendencies.

Their version of the quantity theory was refined and given more logical precision. Money, regarded as a medium of exchange, must be defined as including everything used for that purpose – not merely gold, silver, and paper money but also bank deposits. Whenever an exchange of goods or services for dollars takes place, the exchange constitutes use of money, or a "transaction." Now, if the circulation of money changes in the same proportion as the number of transactions, the level of average prices must remain the same. If circulation increases more rapidly than transactions, prices will rise, and vice versa. Circulation, in turn, results both from the amount *of money in use and from the* velocity *with which it passes from hand to hand.*

All this was mathematically expressed in Irving Fisher's celebrated equation of exchange, the simplest form of which is, as first written by Simon Newcomb,

$$MV = PT$$

where, at any given time, M *is the quantity of money,* V *the velocity of its circulation,* P *the general price level, and* T *the number of transactions.*

In the eyes of the stable-money theorists, M *was the controllable factor of this equation and* P *the factor which it was important to keep constant. Therefore deliberate changes in* M *ought to be made to counterbalance any changes that might occur in* V *and* T. *Suppose, for example, that as the country grew, the number of transactions doubled while the velocity of circulation remained the same. In that case, thought Fisher, the quantity of money ought also to be doubled.*[3]

A variation of this equation is $P = \dfrac{MV}{T}$. It is obvious that if the money supply M is fixed or rigid and if the velocity of circulation V is assumed constant, then prices P must decline as economic activity T expands.

Assuming the same conditions, we see mathematically that as production tends toward infinity, prices must tend toward zero. As I stated earlier, however, many prices are fixed by statute or contract and do not decline as production increases. (This point will be explored more fully later.) Under these circumstances, with a fixed money supply, production will be artificially restricted, recession will set in and unemployment will rise.

All this may seem innocent enough to the unsuspecting layman, but at the point where Fisher began to advocate deliberate management of the quantity of money he ran smack into conservative orthodoxy. The amount of bank money was supposed to be dependent in the first instance on the free play

of profit-seeking among competitive banks and those who bor-
rowed from them, and ultimately on the gold reserve. As for
government-issued paper money, the government's only duty
was to keep it "sound" by making sure that every Treasury note
or certificate could be exchanged for a permanently fixed weight
of monetary metal. Yet Fisher wanted to vary that weight as
prices went up or down, so that a dollar, instead of buying an
invariable amount of gold, would, he thought, buy an invariable
amount of commodities.

He assumed, in accordance with classical reasoning, that
to make the dollar worth less or more in gold would automati-
cally change the quantity of money in circulation. But his sug-
gested shackling of the "invisible hand", or natural law, which
was supposed to arrange all things for the best if only there were
no interference, was thought by the orthodox highly dangerous,
not to say impious.[4]

The "new theology" was still smothered by economic orthodoxy and the perennial problem persisted.

It was not until John Maynard Keynes challenged the conventional wisdom that the "professionals" began to question the
classical assumptions. Ricardian orthodoxy had not been seriously challenged for more than a century since Malthus. The
latter had been aware of the shortage of purchasing power by
simply observing the obvious. Because he was unable to explain in detail how this shortage arose, however, he was unable
to dent the classical fortress.

Ricardo conquered England as completely as the Holy In-
quisition conquered Spain. Not only was his theory accepted by
the city, by statesmen and by the academic world. But contro-
versy ceased; the other point of view completely disappeared;
it ceased to be discussed.[5]

Keynes was amazed at this phenomenon. An important issue
was ignored completely by economic writers and only lived on
"furtively, below the surface."

Keynes knew instinctively that something was wrong. His
major work, *The General Theory of Employment, Interest and*
Money, was dedicated to "a struggle of escape from habitual
modes of thought and expression."[6] It was addressed primarily

to his fellow economists who, he felt, were subject to an increasing credibility gap due to the signal failure of their reigning orthodoxy for purposes of scientific prediction.

For professional economists, after Malthus, were apparently unmoved by the lack of correspondence between the results of their theory and the facts of observation; — a discrepancy which the ordinary man has not failed to observe, with the result of his growing unwillingness to accord to economists that measure of respect which he gives to other groups of scientists whose theoretical results are confirmed by observation when they are applied to the facts.[7]

Keynes realized that a periodic shortage of aggregate demand was a real problem. He could not understand why it had been dismissed so summarily by the classical economists. He argued that the key to understanding the periodic shortages of aggregate demand was an insufficiency of investment spending based on businessmen's views of the future. Recessions were not caused by a rising demand for money, he suggested, but "a more typical, and often the predominant explanation of the crisis is, not primarily a rise in the rate of interest, but a sudden collapse in the marginal efficiency of capital."[8]

Keynes also recognized that trade unions were reluctant to accept reductions in money wages and when investment spending collapsed unemployment was the result. A fall in the rate of interest would not be too helpful because a businessman who could not already sell his existing production profitably would probably not want to borrow to increase his manufacturing capacity.

Implicit in Keynes' general theory is an acceptance of the inevitability of the business cycle. Keynes' remedy for this situation called for direct government action through fiscal policy to alter the level of aggregate demand. When investment is inadequate and unused resources are available, government should borrow from individuals or the banks and embark on its own investment programme. This will provide jobs and income and, through the multiplier effect, a powerful economic stimulus. Alternatively, when an economy is overheated and all of its resources are occupied, government can raise, through taxation, more money than it needs for its expenditures, both current and investment.

This general approach has been adopted by almost all British economists as well as by many foreign practitioners. Its adoption has been generally credited with the avoidance, in the Western private capital countries, of the serious recession or depression forecast for the postwar years. It introduced an element of humanity into monetary management. In future, reasonably full employment would be a constant goal. Helpless workers would no longer be the unwilling pawns of financial orthodoxy.

The considerable success enjoyed by Keynesian economists rests largely on the fact that much government borrowing has been through the banking system. Inevitably, to facilitate this borrowing on the scale required, central banks have been obliged to augment the supply of money considerably. Through this system, sufficient aggregate demand (sometimes too much) has been created to finance rapid economic growth. Government expenditures of money borrowed in this way have not been limited to investment but have often included current consumption as well. In the short run, it does not really matter. An important, even critical, gap had been filled and adequate aggregate demand was available consistently, as required.

The method of putting new money into circulation must be one of the seven wonders of the world. Governments issue bonds which they sell to the public and the banks for cash. Then when they want to increase the money supply, the Central Bank buys back some of the bonds for newly-printed paper money. This new money, cash, finds its way into the banking system and, on the basis of increased cash reserves, the banks are able to increase their loans to customers substantially. They also become potential buyers of additional government bonds.

If a task force were set up to find a rational, equitable way of putting new money into circulation, and if it reported as a solution the present practice, it would be laughed out of court or, possibly, its members would be unceremoniously drowned. But the system works because we have a fractional reserve banking system. If our banks were required to hold 100 per cent reserves, it would not work. Although there are alternatives which might be studied, the present system can continue to work as long as governments are prepared to provide immediate massive liquidity (printed money) in the event of temporary loss of public confidence.[9]

Complicated as the tools have been, postwar progress in understanding economic issues has been phenomenal. There is no further talk of "imminent collapse" of the "capitalist" system. Massive unemployment comparable to that of the 1930's is a thing of the past. The techniques of monetary and fiscal management for growth are quite well understood. (It is not necessary for me to discuss these techniques here because several extensive and excellent works are already available.)[10] The problems that remain are serious but certainly no more serious than the problems we have solved. Private capital systems, though hardly ideal, are evolving toward performance that compares most favourably with the state capital alternatives.

The developments described in these first chapters suggest two main conclusions to me. First, what men *think* about economics is a crucial determinant of what happens. Poor theory precedes poor performance. Conversely, better performance requires better theory. Second, the "open" system with all its faults does have the compensating virtue of being able to learn; albeit slowly, but learn nevertheless.

Without completely accepting Keynes' general theory and notwithstanding his implied recognition of the inevitability of business cycles, which I reject completely, I believe he has made an essential contribution to society and must be given much credit for the dynamic postwar thrust. He has forced professional economists to climb down from their sterile platforms and to try new solutions. It pains me to observe, however, that it was not the validity of his theory alone that made the impact. It was also his credentials. Keynes was a recognized member of the club.

Notes

1. For budget discussion see U.K. Parliamentary Debates, Vol. clxxxiii, col. 55.
2. R. Craig McIvor, *Canadian Monetary Banking and Fiscal Development*, (Toronto: The Macmillan Company of Canada Limited, 1958), p. 160.
3. Soule, *Ideas of the Great Economists*, p. 111.
4. *Ibid.*, p. 112.
5. J.M. Keynes, *The General Theory of Employment, Interest and Money*, (London: 1960), Macmillan & Co. Ltd., and St. Martin's Press, Inc., p. 32.
6. *Ibid.*
7. *Ibid.*, p. 33.
8. *Ibid.*, p. 315.
9. I was tempted to do a chapter on this fascinating subject but decided against it because I do not want to get off the trail chasing rabbits in the middle of a moose hunt.
10. See, for example, Walter Heller ed., *Perspectives on Economic Growth*, (New York: Random House, 1968). Naturally I have reservations about some of the views expressed.

Chapter 3

A Case Study:
The Japanese Experience

It is always dangerous and perhaps unwise to single out any one country for special mention. Yet, in reviewing the evolution of the private capital system, I feel compelled to cite the case of Japan whose postwar experience in economic management has been so exceptional that it is almost unique. A book on political economy that omitted up-to-date information on Japan would be of questionable value. It was the best of good fortune, then, that allowed me to verify my written material on the spot in a delightful visit that included some of the most candid and interesting interviews of my whole research.

In response to a telegram from Canberra, my hosts had booked a seat on the "bullet," the high-speed dayliner from Tokyo to Osaka where I would be met by Mr. Patrick Reid, the Canadian Commissioner to EXPO 70. My guide took me to the station platform a few minutes before train time. An elevated sign indicated where passengers for car No. 8 should assemble and an arrow on the platform floor indicated the centre line for the queue. Soon the train arrived. The double door opened exactly in line with the painted arrow. Passengers filed in quickly and were soon seated in the appropriate places. As the second hand on the station clock left 8:59:50 and approached 9:00:00, the train began to move, gently but powerfully.

My brief glimpse of Japanese life outside the great metropolis was fascinating. Although there were sights and sounds of mechanization, much of the old tradition was visible. Farmers worked in their paddies, people worked and played in traditional and modern garb. Low clouds hid the snow-capped peak of Fujiama, one of the few landmarks well known to foreigners.

As the train rolled on, my attention often passed from outside to inside. Attractive girls passed by with cartloads of gaily coloured delicacies. Chocolates, candies, soft drinks and box lunches were available. The man ahead bought two lunches and began the dual mission of eating and teaching his small son the fine art of trainboard chopstick management. The father was very skilful and the son was very attentive.

As we approached Osaka, I heard my name being called. I was wanted on the telephone. On the telephone? A conductor, recognizing my puzzlement, motioned toward the rear. The doors between cars opened automatically for me. (None of the pushing and leaning and lurching that I remembered from my train-riding days on the Ottawa-Toronto run). In the buffet car, a pretty girl pointed to telephone cubicle No. 1 and said that she would connect me immediately. A moment later, Mr. Reid was on the line cautioning me not to get off at the wrong station. He vigorously denied my suggestion that he was really trying to demonstrate the superiority of the Japanese communication system.

A few minutes later, the bullet began to slow down. The station came into view. At exactly 12:10:00 we stopped. The trip of 300 miles had taken 3 hours and 10 minutes, exactly as scheduled. Tall and handsome and Irish, Patrick Reid was there to greet me. After a pleasant luncheon, he was to take me on a tour of the soon to be opened EXPO 70 and our own magnificent Canadian Pavilion. The biggest and most universally participated-in world exposition was the first to be built in Asia – a great tribute to the Japanese people.

The accomplishments of Japan are the more remarkable when one recalls the extensive destruction of her economy during World War II. Six years after the war, the peace treaty was signed and production reached pre-war levels. Since then, it has taken further giant strides. The growth rate has been exceptionally rapid. Price stability has been less than satisfactory but perhaps reasonable for a period of high growth. Periodic exchange crises have tested the government's will to maintain the external value of its currency. On balance, the performance has been amazing.

Japanese experts are tolerantly amused at the foreigner's request to explain what is happening. Rather than to pretend that I am the expert, I will merely pass on the explanations of economic performance given to me by Japanese bankers, government officials, and union leaders. I have no reason to think that these are not basically true.

Economic Planning and Management

The principal determinants of the Japanese postwar economic performance were good planning in economic management, high capital formation, the Japanese people themselves and their attitude toward work and, finally, political stability. Without attempting to set any order of importance, I would like to discuss each of these factors in turn.

Economic planning in Japan is "indicative" rather than regulatory. The system is a privately administered capital system. It is not a planned socialist economy. Consequently, the government's five-year plans do not prescribe economic activities in detail. At least that is true for the private sector. Naturally, the government will follow its own plan for the public sector as faithfully as possible. For private business, the plan describes only the general direction that development should follow, subject, of course, to any action that the government may take to induce or encourage industry to conform. Although the government claims few direct means to intervene and influence the economy, the plan does have considerable influence on business intentions and decision-making, especially in respect to capital investment, and it helps to maintain business confidence in future trends.

The economic growth rate forecast in each of the five-year

plans has always been lower than the actual rate achieved previously. Conservative planning avoids serious risk of overheating or creating imbalances. On the other hand, business confidence, which has been consistently "bullish," generated the motive power necessary for rapid growth.

One of the sharp contrasts between Japanese practice and Canadian practice is the degree of cooperation between government and business. Again and again, Japanese officials told me they would not think of introducing major changes in policy without first consulting business. There is a harmony of purpose in Japan between government and industry that is lacking, in varying degrees, in other countries, including my own. The Japanese government wants business to be successful because that is consistent with national objectives. In some countries, business is considered intrinsically evil and, therefore, a fit object of obstruction, control and distrust. There is no doubt in my mind that this partnership approach produces the best results.

The Japanese have been successful in demand management. This is fundamental, of course, to a full employment, rapid growth policy. The principal tools are fiscal and monetary measures with primary emphasis, at least initially, on the latter. This has resulted in the high level of savings being employed profitably.

The cooperation and support of the central bank is absolutely essential to effective demand management. The Bank of Japan has cooperated fully. Interestingly enough, Japan was the only country I visited whose officials unashamedly and unhesitatingly volunteered the information: "We have a managed currency." Most countries do but many are reluctant to admit it. The Japanese manage their currency and manage it very successfully. The results speak for themselves. They do not claim to have solved all of the intricate problems associated with demand management but they do profess a willingness to experiment with new techniques as circumstances require. That is a fresh and heartening approach.

Policy objectives have emphasized the ideal of full employment and maximum growth consistent with reasonable price stability. Recently consumer prices have been rising at an annual rate of about 6 per cent, which is high but not out of line with some other industrialized countries. Despite this inflation, the Japanese real growth rate remains very high. In short, both economic planning and economic management in Japan look good.

High Capital Formation

Unless it calls for and encourages a reasonable rate of capital formation (imports aside), no economic plan will succeed in promoting a high rate of growth. The Japanese are well aware of the relationship between capital goods and growth. As their incomes increased, the savings ratio rose sharply. In 1952, according to the Bank of Japan, when per capita GNP was only $204 (U.S.), the savings ratio was an astonishingly high 21 per cent. In 1969, with a per capita GNP of approximately $1,600 (U.S.), the savings level was forecast at a remarkable 37 per cent! This is far above the level of other industrialized countries and must be one of the principal reasons for Japan's superior economic performance. As in other growth-oriented countries, the acceleration of savings gives rise to an acceleration of growth of GNP, which in turn results in even higher savings ratios.

Why are Japanese savings so high? Many explanations are offered. It may reflect the culture of the Japanese people who respect the traditional virtue of frugality. The absence of universal social welfare schemes may foster a desire for greater self-protection through accumulated savings. The encouragement and tax advantages provided by government may be contributing factors. Whatever the reasons, the savings level is extremely high and still rising. Even with changing priorities for investment, a continued high rate of growth seems assured.

The government, realizing the importance of this national characteristic to the fulfillment of its economic plans, is willing to take extraordinary measures to maintain confidence in the banking system and other repositories of the people's savings. In 1966, a crash and near panic on the Japanese stock market and a run on mutual funds put some of the larger securities companies on the verge of bankruptcy. The government, the Bank of Japan and the leading banks saved the situation and provided the necessary liquidity to the endangered institutions. Some governments and central banks might consider the Japanese action highly unorthodox. Perhaps it was, but it was also eminently sensible. The credibility of the institutions and of the stock market was maintained as a legitimate and recognized channel for accumulated savings.

The most popular form of savings is a bank deposit or a government post office savings deposit paying 5 to 5.5 per cent interest. For an outsider, this is remarkable in view of the long term inflation rate of 5 to 6 per cent. The Japanese must have great confidence in their currency and economic system not to seek more rewarding investments. Any doubt as to how long this can persist is offset by noting that it has been going on for years.

The Japanese People

Any discussion of Japan's economic performance that neglected the basic character and deeply rooted traditions of the Japanese people would be grossly incomplete. For the Japanese there is something almost sacred about work and about the concept of contributing. These tie in with the family, the influence of which permeates Japanese society.

Robert Ballon discusses the family-like nature of Japanese industrial enterprise, emphasizing that "the employee, rather than being hired, was adopted as a member of the family, his participation entailing grounds larger than his actual individual contribution of skill or performance, more generally, that of a human resource."[1]

Employment is for life. After an initial period, an employee is considered hired and stays with his company until retirement. The company provides its employees with many fringe benefits which often include subsidized housing and invariably include retirement benefits. Unions are organized on a company basis. Life tenure makes collective agreements of the "western" style inappropriate. Usually there is a high degree of cooperation between management and union. This is sometimes demonstrated at fairs or gatherings where employees sing company songs.

This stability and application to work must be a strong force in industrial growth. Because individuals are hired as universalists – a human resource – rather than as specialists, they are quite willing to undertake any task assigned. They are not as concerned about the type of job they are doing as they are about the geographical location of the plant to which they are assigned. Thus within the structure of the industrial empire of their company, they are a "fluid" resource, and easily adaptable to new demands and new developments.

When I was in Japan, I was informed that the workers had just turned down the five-day week in favour of retention of the five and one half day week. This was interesting because it illustrated the general attitude toward work, and because it indicated that the Japanese understand basic economies. They knew they could not cut the work week by nine per cent and still have the same real income. They chose income.

Political Stability

There is no doubt that the relative political stability in Japan during the postwar years has been an important factor contributing to the high and stable growth of the economy. Stable government, however, is often the corollary of economic success. If it acts wisely and if its policies contribute to conditions of full employment, high growth and an equitable distribution, government will likely hold the confidence of the electorate. The confidence of the electorate produces majority governments that are able to take courageous, though sometimes unpopular action, being assured that the long term results will be recognized as beneficial. Japanese governments have planned wisely and, when necessary, courageously.

No doubt increased expenditures in the public domain will affect the growth rate. But the economic base is so strong and the capital formation rate so high that a considerable shift in resources can take place without impeding growth. The economic roots are so strong that the branches can spread considerably without danger of imbalance.

Changes in attitude, however, are occurring. The younger Japanese are not as firmly wedded to the lifetime employment concept as their elders are. They possess greater skills and want earlier and more substantial recognition for them. The older generation, whose seniority and preferred position would be threatened by such a fundamental change, can be expected to resist strongly and resolutely. Over the years, nevertheless, some change is bound to occur.

There is also the problem of inflation. Japan's rate has been consistently high for a number of years, but the burden of inflation has been distributed fairly evenly among the working groups. Consequently, as long as it has not interfered with Japan's competitive position in world markets, it has been accepted with equanimity. It would be a matter of greater concern if millions of small Japanese investors awoke to the reality of the zero return, in real terms, that they are getting on their savings deposits. At least the Japanese understand what is causing their inflation. Very high wage increases in capital intensive industries are offset by equally high gains in productivity. But wage increases in service industries are not offset by gains in productivity. The result is higher costs and higher prices.

As I left Japan, I could not escape the feeling that here was a country on the way up. The reservations I have mentioned are relatively few and, in the main, the dangers relatively remote. Here is a country with a sense of purpose and a basic harmony between its peoples. Student activists, yes. A few marxists, yes. But the overwhelming majority are satisfied with the progress they are making and determined that it will continue. I have no doubt that it will.

Notes

1. Robert J. Ballon, *The Japanese Employee*. Tokyo: Sophia University, and Vermont: Charles E. Tuttle Co. (1969).

PART TWO

Socialism:
The State-Capital
Approach

Chapter 4

A New Approach?

When I mentioned to some of my friends that I was going to write a book with an updated view of liberalism, one or two suggested that it contain a system for "enlightened" people. My friends were idealists who felt strongly that our present system is inadequate in many ways and that our only hope is a civilization based on a new and improved order.

I admit that the suggestion to pursue this course was tempting. Like my friends, and many others, I have long been dissatisfied with the social order. Observation leaves little doubt that most of the world's problems are caused by people, their institutions and the relationships between them. From this comes a fundamental urge to establish a model society based on a new, and very old, view of human potential.

A bit of quiet reflection brought me back to earth. One thing I have learned during my years in public life is that progress is slow and that politics is the "art of the possible." People are not perfect! People are people! In rereading parts of the Old Testament, it seems to me that although we have made some social progress since those days it has been a modest gain. Attitudes and practices have changed but human nature has not changed measurably.

The early socialists and, later, Marx constructed systems based on the "perfectability" of man. These systems envisaged men of goodwill building a world of economic and social equality hitherto unknown. Egalitarianism would prevail in a new natural order based on the tenet that Marx borrowed from Louis Blanc: "From each according to his ability, to each according to his needs." This would permit maximum economic and social development based on a desire by the individual not to pursue his own ends but to seek satisfaction and fulfillment in contributing to the needs of others. What decent man can fail to be moved by such an ideal? Is there, however, sufficient altruism in the world to make such a system work?

Certainly, I can think of few souls who would meet the high standards required. Politics brings one into direct contact with thousands of people as counsellor, friend, advocate, pleader, father confessor, and opponent. It is a wonderful way to learn about human nature, not from text books, but from experience. One sees much of the seamy side of human nature and, from time to time, something of its nobility. The scoreboard would be a caution to anyone designing a social and economic system that relied for its success primarily on the unselfishness of the vast majority of its participants. This "not so nice" observation has been corroborated by a number of my contemporaries. One is driven to the conclusion, albeit most reluctantly, that any social and economic system must take into account the weaknesses as well as the strengths of human nature. My caution is reinforced by my primary concern with the human suffering and misery that can be relieved in the next decade or two. A hundred years hence there may be "a whole new ball game." If there is, the generation then living can make the necessary adjustments.

Many people who say that they would be willing to contribute according to their ability and only take what they need fail to pass a particular test; that is, when you introduce into the conversation a reference to their own circumstances and to persons in immediate competition with them the idealism becomes increasingly evasive and defensive. Men may wish mankind well and yet be very reluctant to make the first personal sacrifice. Perhaps the best illustration of this from my own experience is the case of those socialist millionaires who are quite willing to distribute other people's wealth to the poor but who seldom make the convincing gesture of starting with the unilateral distribution of their own.

If I interpret the facts correctly, the day-to-day expression of human nature is at a much lower plane than we would like to think. My guess, and it is only a guess, though based on considerable experience, is that perhaps two or three per cent of the people I meet would follow the principle "from each according to his ability, to each according to his needs." I mean this judgment to apply in the context of a long term and voluntary situation, not, of course, in a short term and emotional situation. There is no doubt that people can and will work cooperatively and harmoniously for a short term, in face of an emergency either real or imagined. It is in these circumstances that men achieve their highest ideals through acts of heroism and unselfishness. Once the crisis is over, however, regression sets in.

Consider a hypothetical situation in which several survivors of an accident at sea reach the safety of a deserted island. One is assigned the task of building and maintaining a fire, a second of building an adequate shelter and a third must fish. There is complete harmony and cooperation in the group. Cheerfulness is the order of the day and there is no suggestion that one task is more important than another or that one survivor is producing more effectively than a brother.

A week passes and the shelter is complete, including roughly-hewn but relatively comfortable furniture. The builder then decides to make a flute to provide some entertainment. This is well received at first. A couple of days later, however, the supply of fish declines and the fisherman must put in longer hours with poorer results. The sound of the flute begins to take on an irritating tone. That evening, the fisherman makes a sarcastic comment and the next day lays down an ultimatum. "If you don't leave that damn flute alone and help with the food supply, you won't get any."

If you don't like my story, make up your own. Anyone

who has spent a week on a camping trip or assisted regularly with turkey dinners provided by the women's auxiliary of the local church can give you one from their experience.

There are examples where large groups of people have worked together for extended periods in the achievement of national goals. Certainly this happened during World War II. The benefits were not distributed strictly on a basis of need but the amount of unselfish work performed on a completely voluntary basis was phenomenal. It is an irony that when man is engaged in his basest pursuit, war, great acts of dedication and sacrifice are performed. (Of course, this dedication is usually reinforced by repeated doses of highly emotional propaganda.)

This strong motivation is difficult to maintain for prolonged periods in peacetime. Special appeals are made but they are usually of short duration. Some of the state capital countries have tried sustained appeals with some success. This involves invoking a form of warfare, the cold war, in which the honour of the nation's performance in competition with other nations is at stake. For reasonable success, repeated appeals to patriotism are required and a controlled press is a virtual necessity. Even then, it is difficult to maintain the fervour. People tend to regress to being "human," a fact witnessed by the results in the USSR and its eastern European satellites.

Any examples of prolonged group devotion are mainly special cases. The Mennonite and Hutterite groups, familiar to Canadians living in Ontario, Manitoba, Saskatchewan, Alberta and British Columbia, have developed forms of cooperative living that please the members of the groups involved and, although not universally popular in the outside community, are generally tolerated.

There are many variations within the Mennonite religion. Perhaps the most important is between the Eastern Mennonites, who are descendants of Pennsylvania Germans of South German and Swiss origin, and the Western Mennonites, who came directly to Canada from Europe. Despite internal tension between conservative and liberal, traditional and modern views, these groups share many general similarities. There is a common evangelical and biblical emphasis. Most groups are anti-modern and refuse to become involved in public affairs outside the circle. Basically pacifist, they follow a strict, personal, moral code and a simple and frugal life-style. Not surprisingly, the groups are exclusivist and marrying outside the community is forbidden on pain of excommunication.

The great majority of the Hutterites are descendants of Austrian peasants. Many of these migrated to Canada from the United States because of persecution in World War I for their conscientious-objector status. There have been similar, if less serious, frictions in Canada. They are even more exclusive than the Mennonites, partly because of a history of real or perceived persecution. (Their book of Martyrs runs to 1500 graphic pages.) Their life-style is a form of Christian collectivism based on the philosophy that all God's spiritual and material gifts are given to man that he may share them with his fellow men. "Communities of Brethern" consist of one to two hundred souls. No one has personal property, but there is a strong work ethic with job rotation strictly supervised by democratically elected household heads. Large families live in small apartments. Marriage takes place early – men, 21; women, 19 – and mates are normally chosen from another Hutterite community. Schooling is rarely pursued beyond grade six due to a considerable suspicion of "learning."

An atmosphere of sociability exists and there is much visiting back and forth. Doors are not locked and knocking is considered unnecessary. A strong concept of solidarity exists, but this internal solidarity is paralleled by a rigid exclusion of the outside world.

The Israeli *kibbutz* is yet another example of relatively successful communal living. The *kibbutz* is still a charismatic institution in Israel and evokes strong reactions, both pro and con. It has been the embodiment of the Zionist ideal and an instrument in refashioning the image of the Jew. Agriculturally, in making the desert bloom, it has contributed to the fulfillment of prophecy. The *kibbutz* is labour intensive and community centered and, thus, an excellent source of employment and orientation for the many European immigrants. It plays an important defence role, particularly in border areas. In carrying out these functions under extreme conditions, the *kibbutz* has contributed enormously to the military and political leadership of Israel.

But there is evidence of change, some of it very painful.

Many of the original functions have been taken over by the national civil and military bureaucracy. The ideological focus of attention has also shifted from the *kibbutz* to the state. Its image as the pioneering idealistic agent of agrarian development has been eroded somewhat by the relative prosperity of many of its members. The development of managerial specialization has affected the spirit of community labour.

Changes have also occurred in the "social communism" of the *kibbutz*. For example, many second generation parents have wanted a greater role in the upbringing and education of their children. Conflict arises with respect to specially-gifted children. The interest of the child and, perhaps, of the State as a whole may be in conflict with those of the *kibbutz*. Too much education can result in underutilization on the *kibbutz,* or loss of the individual to the cities. All masters cannot be equally served. Outside labour, including foreign labour, is required to harvest crops. The result of all this has been a painful re-evaluation of the nature and functions of the *kibbutz* within the State of Israel. It has prospered in the highly-emotional atmosphere of reclaiming an ancient territory and the establishment or re-establishment of a nation state on "sacred ground." There is no guarantee that succeeding generations will be content with the discipline of conformity once the "crisis" of survival has passed and the existence of statehood and independence recognized.

Though there have been some notable exceptions, usually within small groups, the success stories in the field of cooperative living are rare. Many experiments, which on the surface, at least, were revolts[1] against the spirit of gain or private acquisition, ended in failure. Such an experiment were the "Phalanxes" organized by the disciples of Charles Fourier.[2]

In theory, socialism is a great ideal. In practice, on a major scale, it just will not work. People have not reached that stage of evolution where they are consistently willing to subordinate their own interests to the interests of other, sometimes less deserving, people. Any realistic political system must consider the observable behaviour of its participant peoples. One is driven to accept Max Weber's admonition that "it is precisely the ethics of responsibility to take into account the average deficiencies of men."

Notes

1. Most of these alternatives were really a reaction to the historical circumstances which appeared, at the time, rather hopeless.
2. From *Ideas of the Great Economists* by George Soule. Copyright © 1952 by George Soule. All rights reserved. Reprinted by permission of The Viking Press, Inc.

Chapter 5

People Cheat

An obvious manifestation of the "average deficiencies of men" is the fact that people cheat. It is unpleasant to say this and I realize that the statement may be offensive. I have searched for neutral terms such as "self-interest" to describe the phenomenon but they are not quite accurate. The fact is that people do cheat.

Almost all children steal at some point in their development. No doubt, opportunity is an important factor in this. This tendency in children passes quickly or slowly depending on the reaction and attitude of parents and other adults. The remarkable and fortunate thing is that most children are taught and subsequently live by a quite high standard of honesty. Everyone, however, allows himself a certain tolerance. We all cheat sometimes and think it acceptable.

Most adults will not cheat on the small store owner. The act is too personal and direct, the violation of the golden rule too obvious. Cheating little people "face to face" is unacceptable behaviour. This taboo is relaxed somewhat in proportion to the size of the enterprise. When I was in the building business, I observed the tendency of some home purchasers to collect unused bricks or lumber from the building site and store these in their basements. The amounts were not large. They might vary, in dollar value, from $5 to $100. Obviously someone thought that the materials might come in handy later for the construction of a barbecue, or to finish a basement recreation area. Even though the value of materials taken was not great, the increase in cost was often significant. Lumber was delivered in package lots, exactly right for the unit being built. Loss of one joist or one rafter could hold up the production line for several hours and, sometimes, if re-scheduling of work crews was necessary, by a day or two. The resulting increase in cost was considerable. Not realizing the side effects of their scavenging, the customers rationalized their behaviour by pretending that they had already paid for it. Surplus materials were assumed to be included in the bill. In fact, home buyers as a group had to pay for the extra cost of cheating. It would have been more economical to buy what they needed when they needed it.

Although the construction company I have referred to was not large in terms of business enterprises, it was just large enough to be impersonal. Really big organizations have even higher losses. Some people who would not have cheated us would not be too concerned about a bit of petty larceny if Eatons, Macys or Sears were involved. "They are so big they would never notice it," is a common attitude. This attitude is even more marked in reference to U.S. Steel, General Motors, Ford or Dupont. Few of us would worry if a friend or acquaintance stole a wrench or a few nuts and bolts from one of those. They are big. They are wealthy. They would be financially unaffected by small losses.

The scale rises further when it comes to governments. Most people think the government is fair game. It is so big and so impersonal. Few people realize that it is really themselves they are cheating. The most common offence is at customs. Smuggling is a form of sport. For most, it is penny ante, just a few small knick-knacks or a couple of packages of undeclared cigarettes. Others are more daring. Nor is this cheating proportional to the need of the individual. Quite often it is just the opposite.

A few years ago my wife and I attended a conference of Public Housing Authorities of Ontario held at Niagara Falls, Ontario. During the male deliberations, the ladies arranged a visit to Niagara Falls, New York. One of the ladies, the wife of a senior government official, bought a complete outfit and wore it back across the border. No doubt she was expressing her personal interpretation of "to each according to his needs." Customs officials were not invited to comment on the interpretation. On another occasion, I was a member of a group touring the St. Lawrence Seaway while it was under construction. For an amateur, one of the most spectacular sights was the coffer dam which had been built to divert the river while the power dam at Cornwall was being constructed. Even more exciting was the bus trip across the coffer dam to the American side. There were no customs or other formalities due to the high level and sponsored nature of the group. We were there only a few minutes but even that was long enough for a well-known Toronto business man to buy a bag full of film at American prices.

Only the statute of limitations prevents me from making personal confessions in print. We all offend. Even customs officers have been known to slip back and forth across the border with undeclared booty. Individually, these "bonuses" are pretty small. But over a period of months, the total is quite impressive.

Naturally, the greater the possible savings on a particular article, the greater the incentive to take a chance. Soon after I was elected to the House of Commons, the Canadian Government increased the tax on cigarettes; consequently, the difference between Canadian and American cigarette prices increased significantly. Smuggling increased to such an extent that Canadian sales fell below forecasts and the government actually took in less tax revenue than previously. In the next budget, the tax was reduced, sales increased, and governmental revenues rose.

Income tax is another sports arena. Nearly everyone takes advantage of all the loopholes legally available to him. A much smaller but still significant group go beyond the legal loopholes. When I was in business, I knew an accountant (not the one who kept the company books) who kept telling me that the company was paying too much tax. Our expenses were not high enough. This was difficult for me to comprehend because I thought our expenses were high enough. I suspected, correctly as it turned out, that he was suggesting something a bit shady. The next time I heard of him was a few years later when he was arrested for income tax evasion. He had been involved in a scheme which included writing phony invoices. In that most direct way, "expenses" had been increased and a very clever and charming man wound up in jail.

Another area of cheating is welfare. Certainly, many of the people who live on welfare are themselves the victims of large-scale and small-scale cheating. But here as elsewhere there are exploitative attitudes. As welfare payments move toward levels that equal or exceed some wages, the exploitation becomes more systematic. This problem is a serious one for any society that generates poverty.

There is also that new area of exploitability, unemployment insurance. Again citing the Canadian example, the rules say a person must be fired or laid off to qualify for payments. There are hundreds of people who quit their jobs and then ask for and receive from their employers a letter saying they were laid off. This double immorality then qualifies the "unemployed" worker for a paid holiday, often of extended duration. He rationalizes his position by saying that it is his money; he has paid into the fund for years and never drawn a cent. This attitude assumes that the fund is a savings plan rather than an insurance fund. Most people really know the difference, but ease their conscience by believing what they want to believe.

Other raids on the Unemployment Insurance Fund are legal but highly questionable. There are many cases of men and women who earn good incomes from seasonal employment and who then claim unemployment insurance in the off season. I cite the case of the lobster fisherman who earned $22,000 during the season and then drew Unemployment Insurance all winter. There was the case of the civil servant's wife who worked as a secretary at the House of Commons and then drew Unemployment Insurance during the summer recess. These are examples of abuse that is permitted and encouraged by sloppy legislation. Unfortunately, the hidden cost is usually paid (in the form of higher premiums) by people with very modest incomes who work all their lives.

The list of examples I have used is partial and merely for purposes of illustration. It is related to Canadian experience, but would apply to the United States as well. Some other countries are even worse, with cheating virtually a cultural characteristic. Others are much better. Japan seems to me to be an example of a society that cheats less than the average. It appears to me that there is a direct correlation between the progress of a country (at any particular time) and the incorruptibility of its people as reflected in its public men.

It appears that the morals of any civilization move through cycles. They are influenced to a marked degree by leadership. There are always people busily engaged in trying to corrupt any culture. There are always some others fighting corruption at the low end of the cycle. As always, until a new consensus is formed, the fighters will be labelled "cranks."

The purpose of this chapter is not to show that man is intrinsically evil. Nor is it to show that the individual is always the weak link in the social fabric. What is called "cheating" is sometimes only the manifestation of changing values or evidence of bad legislation. In any case, the point is that there is no final and perfect harmony between social and political institutions and the individuals who man these institutions. In designing systems, therefore, it seems wise to have reference to historical man rather than hypothetical man. It seems wise to allow for "weakness." The system which does this will be less likely either to attempt to eradicate sin "finally" through ideological passion or to institutionalize it through absolute power. The tragic irony of "heaven on earth" is that it comes so close to "hell on earth."

The weakness of socialism is that it sees salvation from selfishness in the state. This is one more case of the cure being the ultimate form of the disease. The final result is the perfect impersonality of "Leviathan" and therefore, in my opinion, either wholesale cheating or wholesale repression.

Chapter 6

Public Ownership – The British Case

One of the basic principles of socialism is public ownership. For a long time it was supposed that the corruptive feature of capitalism was private ownership and the ensuing mad scramble for profits. From this ensued the class system of rich and poor, bourgeois and proletariat. The socialist solution to this condition of man pitted against man[1] was the ownership of everything by everyone which, translated into the framework of existing institutions, meant the ownership of everything by the state on behalf of every member of the state. To representative government would be added representative economics.

However much one may sympathize with these aspirations, it is undeniable that the ideas themselves have come upon hard times. The doctrine of public ownership now faces a mass of debilitating evidence. First, there is the unavoidable fact of the Soviet Union, the worker's paradise lost. Second, the concept of representative ownership now appears somewhat naive. The idea that the average man's interests are automatically enhanced by state power has, to say the least, not been proved.

Third, it is now recognized that the essential characteristics of large-scale enterprise remain whether it is "officially" owned by private shareholders or by the public through its proxy politicians. In either case, there exist the requirements of managerial practice. In addition, alternative methods of public control over the economy, which render public ownership anachronistic, have been developed. More will be said on these matters later. It is sufficient to note here the inescapable conclusion that public ownership is usually not worth the trouble.

That the doctrine of public ownership should have suffered the same fate as the doctrine of perfect competition is no coincidence. In both cases, analysis was based on an obsolete view of capitalist society. The doctrinaire anti-monopolists regarded cutthroat competition as the norm. Socialism assumed the same thing about capitalism while drawing opposite conclusions about its desirability. And while all of this assuming was going on, the economic order was changing profoundly in ways that had little to do with either doctrine.

When I argue that these ideas are dead or dying, I am speaking of them as "doctrines." That is, they no longer enjoy an ideological monopoly as principles that are self-evident. An examination of experience in Britain and Canada will precede some strongly-held convictions based on years of personal observation.

Great Britain

In 1963, nationally-owned productive enterprises accounted for about 12 per cent of the British GNP. The debate surrounding these public corporation continues. The steel industry case generates the most heat. Yet, overall, the most noticeable observation is that a kind of equilibrium has been reached. The nationalizers and anti-nationalizers are both stalled. On the one hand, there is clearly no public passion for more public ownership. On the other hand, an attitude of "leave well enough alone" seems to prevail. Everywhere there are signs of creeping pragmatism. The Conservative Party now judges the issue by the polls. The Labour Party does the same thing and produces cautious documents listing nationalization as only a means, not an end.[2]

This sweet reason is in considerable contrast to the charges and counter-charges of the old days. Yet even then there was a cautious approach. By 1900, British socialism, unlike some of its continental cousins, was firmly committed to an "evolutionary" approach. Nationalization was thought of as a series of priorities beginning with basic industry and gradually working from there. The Conservative Party naturally damned socialism whether of the evolutionary or revolutionary variety. But the political symbiosis of opposites working side by side for years had its effects. As a number of observers have noted, language notwithstanding, the British Conservatives accepted the nationalized industries with remarkably little fuss.[3] In place of the Socialist fear of blood in the streets and businessmen at the barricades, there has been only debate and politics.

This does not mean that there were no real differences. There were and, up to a point, there still are. The Labor Party's pre-war programme for nationalization had several basic tenets. First, was the argument of size. This stated that monopoly power – contrary to laissez-faire principles – had reached the point in certain essential industries (gas, electricity, coal) where public control was necessary. Only in this way could the public interest be protected. Closely related to this point was the argument of efficiency, which rested on the assumption, evidenced by the coal industry, that private monopoly power inevitably became arrogant and slothful, charging more for less. The interesting thing about both these arguments is that they borrowed heavily from the rhetoric of classical laissez-faire (competition, efficiency) in order to implement socialism.[4]

In addition to these eminently respectable economic arguments, there were also the larger and more traditional arguments for the public ownership of all major industries. These included: the abhorrence of the profit motive which, it was supposed, could only be eliminated by nationalization; the belief that good labour relations and industrial democracy would be facilitated by public ownership; and, finally, that the public expropriation of the private capitalist would be a giant step toward income equality. These notions, tempered by the sobering air of practical politics, yielded a list of industries which the Labour Party planned to nationalize and finally did nationalize.[5]

The Conservative Party viewed much of this as rot, in a quite literal sense. It was seen as that invidious advance of state control over private enterprise that was so much feared. And yet there were breaches in the Conservative defence. Some of the nationalized industries had already been in the category of public utilities and conservative governments themselves had experimented in war and peace with public economic organizations. The best example of this and one that was to be used as a model in future was the Port of London Authority created in 1908. Furthermore, there were industries, such as coal, that everyone conceded were in bad shape and where the prospects for massive private initiative were slight. That these considerations had weight with the Conservative Party is suggested by the fact that of all the industries nationalized by Labour after the war, only two — steel and highway freight transportation — have been denationalized by a subsequent Conservative government. And steel was a conspicuously healthy and attractive exception to the general rule.

If it appears from this that the Labour Party has won the battle of nationalization, two amendments should be added. In the first place, several attempts at nationalization have failed. The best known of these is the case of I.C.I., the great chemical corporation. In the second place, the management and performance of the nationalized industries have raised serious difficulties for the socialist point of view.

Much of the dust raised by public ownership has whirled about the issue of management. Principles aside, conservatives argued that it could not work because politicians and civil servants were not businessmen. Lord Haldane struck the oft-repeated note in 1919:

> *Unless you grow up in an atmosphere where it is encouraged, you do not have initiative. That is where the businessman has the strength and the advantage. He is in an atmosphere of initiative. The Civil Servant is not.*[6]

The evidence for the proposition that business was not the same as bureaucracy or politics was overwhelming. The Labour Party had to face it. G. D. H. Cole took a step when he wrote:

Most people nowadays, including the majority of socialists, do appear to hold that the direct conduct of industries through Civil Service departments is not the best method of industrial organization.[7]

It was Herbert Morrison, perhaps more than any other individual, who forced the logic of large-scale enterprise upon the socialist consciousness. Throughout the 1930's, he stressed the importance of efficiency and autonomy for the nationalization programme. Morrison stated that the Board should have autonomy and freedom and indicated that not only should it have responsibility but it should also have responsibility "thrust down its throat."[8]

All of this was only a concession to common sense but it was a very difficult and costly concession to socialism. After all, if business was the root of all evil how could "business management" be granted considerable autonomy? If it was granted such independence, what difference remained between public and private enterprise? Enough difference to justify the cost of nationalization? And most basic of all, did this talk of management mean the abandonment of the early doctrines of industrial democracy? It did, as the history of labour consultation boards makes clear.

In short, to make public ownership work, socialism had to be abandoned — or at least substantially revised. The instrument which this revision finally settled upon was the public corporation, a good example of ideological eugenics.[9] This was by no means a new device nor one confined to Great Britain. It was an attempt, since applied in the most diverse situations, to have the best of both the public and private worlds. Franklin Roosevelt, speaking of the Tennessee Valley Authority, described it (hopefully) as "clothed with the power of government but possessed of the flexibility and initiative of private enterprise."[10] Lord Morrison of Lambeth (formerly Herbert Morrison) enunciated the case for public corporations:

We seek to combine the principle of public accountability of a consciousness on the part of the undertaking that it is working for the nation and not for sectional differences, with the liveliness, initiative and a considerable degree of the freedom of a quick moving and progressive business enterprise.[11]

The working out of that combination has faced – and continues to face – many difficulties. There is the problem of determining the nature and limits of public control. In most cases, the statutes of nationalization have adopted a formula that distinguishes general policy matters – under ministerial and parliamentary control – from day-to-day administration, the responsibility of management.[12]

There are those who doubt the effectiveness or desirability of these controls. The parliamentary question has been described as "casual, capricious, superficial and inconclusive."[13] Granting the lack of good humour in this remark, there is still considerable doubt that parliament can effectively supervise the nationalized industries. Speaking of the triumvirate of board, minister and parliament, one leading authority has concluded:

Parliament, glancing from one to the other like a spectator at a tennis match, does not know whom to blame and is deeply suspicious that something which it ought to know is being concealed.[14]

The minister's relationship to the enterprise has been the occasion for at least equal concern. The problem is that ministers and boards have not observed in practice that neat distinction between general policy matters and day-to-day administration. There have been repeated complaints of "old boy" activities and other unholy and informal goings on. One author has suggested "that one could write a history of public enterprise in this country since 1946 under the title 'The Decline and Fall of the Autonomous Corporation'."[15] Others suggest the title might read, "The Capture of Ministers by Management."

The confusion of who decides what is no greater than the confusion of why it is decided. You will recall that the original reason for the public corporation was dissatisfaction with the logic of private enterprise, especially the axiom of profit.

The public corporation must have a different atmosphere at its board table from that of a shareholders meeting; its board and its officers must regard themselves as the high custodians of the public interest.[16]

Now much as our hearts may respond to the ring of "the public interest," experience suggests that it is a trifle vague. The difficulty is that the profit axiom, aside from being a low and perverse human trait, is also an instrument in the larger task of economizing. It is the most common and conveniently comprehensible way of relating costs and benefits. To denounce it as immoral is one thing. To find a satisfactory substitute is something else. The mere act of making an enterprise public does not solve the problem.

Given the variety of purposes the public corporations have been meant to serve, it is no easy matter to judge their overall performance. Predictably there are strong differences of opinion on this matter. Predictably there has been a certain tendency to see what the observer wishes to see. Conservative spokesmen find the business performance of the nationalized industries rather mediocre. Socialist spokesmen plead circumstances to this and claim that other benefits more than offset examples of commercial mediocrity.

The debate about internal and external efficiencies goes on, though perhaps in a rather diminished way. One recent study of the British Fuel and Power industry advanced the following conclusions:

1. Little careful or systematic research has been done to develop and apply valid yardsticks of performance. In many ways the nationalized industries, like big industry generally, are economic "unknowns."

2. Given the complexity of large-scale enterprise, there is not going to be any simple or single measure of success.

If the public corporations were tiny and faced purely competitive markets, if there were no joint costing problems and if their decisions had no social impact, then a commercial orientation would not be actively inappropriate. But to say this is to show how narrow the suitability of the commercial approach is. Under other, more prevalent, conditions, commercial rules will often be empty or wrong, and policy will necessarily be framed ad hoc for the specific situations.

. . . . . the notion of commercial operation does at least have the merit of requiring that decisions supposedly in the social interest be explicitly justified. But this point has been far overextended in the claim that a commercial orientation will provide

positive guidelines for solving the complex problems of the public corporations.[17]

3. By ordinary economic criteria, the power and fuel industries have not done so badly. For example, there has been less misallocation of resources to, and within, the fuel industries than has been commonly supposed.[18]

This is only one study of one part of nationalization in Great Britain. It suggests that we ought to view performance in a cautious, pragmatic way. For those who, on ideological grounds, hoped for or expected disastrous failure, there is disappointment. The nationalized industries have survived and in a few cases, like the coal industry, they have made considerable gains.

On the other hand, for those who expected nationalization to usher in a new era, there is even greater disappointment. The fact is that public ownership, whether or not it can be justified on pragmatic grounds, has done very little to promote the socialist cause. There is, first of all, the obvious consideration that much of the time these industries have been controlled by Conservative governments. But beyond that, it is clear that they simply are not very different in certain essential respects from any large enterprise. Take the subject of labour relations as an example. It was hoped in the early days that nationalization would create new harmony between labour and management and general improvement in working conditions. The results have disappointed those hopes.

Regarding wages, the nationalized industries have only kept pace with private industry. Railroad wages have lagged behind and coal wages have gained substantially. There has been an across-the-board improvement in miners' working conditions but most observers attribute this to the postwar economics of coal and not to nationalization.[19] Despite that improvement, industrial relations in the coal industry remain, as they have long been, among the worst in Great Britain. Generally speaking, industrial relations are not noticeably better in the public sector than in the private sector. The atmosphere is essentially the same and all the early proposals for worker consultation in managerial decision-making have come to nothing.

Overall, the record of public enterprise is rather dismal for the true-believer. One group within the Labour Party has concluded that "we cannot disguise the fact that the public corporations have not, so far, provided everything which socialists expected from nationalized industries."[20] Another group expanded on the thought:

> *There is a tendency for people at both the red and blue ends of the political spectrum to think that to advocate more and more nationalization is to advocate more and more socialism. Nationalization may be only a convenient slogan to avoid the necessity for new thinking.*[21]

It may well be.

Notes

1. A Current joke has it that whereas in the capitalist west it is a war of man against man, in the Soviet east the opposite holds true.
2. Hugh Gaitskell, "Socialism and Nationalization," Fabian Tract #300, 1956, reprinted in A.H. Hanson, *Nationalization: A Book of Readings*, (Toronto: University of Toronto Press, 1963), pp. 23-31.
3. C.A.R. Crosland, *The Future of Socialism*, (New York: Schocken Books, Inc., 1963), p. 20.
4. *Ibid.*, pp. 312-327.
5. The bundle included the public utilities (gas, electricity and the railroads) as well as coal, steel and basic transport.
6. Hanson, *Nationalization*, p. 78.
7. *Ibid.*, p. 80.
8. A.H. Hanson, *Parliament and Public Ownership*, published for Hansard Society, (London: Cassell, 1961), p. 19.
9. Whether this is a case of cross-fertilization or cross-sterilization remains open to debate.
10. "The Government Corporation," *The Encyclopedia Brittanica*, 1969, V. 10.
11. Lord Morrison, *Government and Parliament*, (London: Oxford University Press, 1964), p. 292.
12. For example, the *Coal Industry Nationalization Act* of 1946 reads that "the minister may after consultation with the [Coal] Board give to the board directions of a general character," quoted in Hanson, *Parliament and Public Ownership*, p. 35.
13. Mr. Hugh Molson quoted in Hanson, *Parliament and Public Ownership*, p. 51.
14. Hanson, *Parliament and Public Ownership*, p. 208.
15. *Ibid.*, p. 175. It has been noted that "Ministers have been taking an increasingly close interest in the finance of the nationalized industries; and government intervention is likely to be a decisive factor in the more important questions of price and wage policies." William A. Robson,

Nationalized Industry and Public Ownership, (London: George Allen and Unwin Ltd., 1962), p. 157.

16. Herbert Morrison, *Socialization and Transport,* (London: Curtis Brown Ltd., 1933), pp. 156-57.
17. William G. Shepherd, *Economic Performance Under Public Ownership: British Fuel and Power*, (New Haven: Yale Studies in Economics, 18, 1965), p. 139.
18. *Ibid.*, p. 140.
19. B.C. Roberts, "Trade Unions and Nationalization," *Progress*, V. 44, No. 245, pp. 114-18, reprinted in Hanson, *Nationalization*, pp. 372-381.
20. "Keeping Left," a statement by twelve M.P.'s normally regarded as "Left Wing," quoted in Crosland, *Future of Socialism*, p. 324.
21. "Social Ownership," a statement by the *Co-operative Movement*, quoted in Crosland, *Future of Socialism*, p. 323.

Chapter 7

Public Ownership
in Canada

Unlike Britain, Canada has never been governed by a socialist party. The New Democratic Party (formerly the Cooperative Commonwealth Federation) has never progressed beyond being a comparatively small third party. This does not mean that socialism has not influenced national policy. Nor does it mean that public ownership has been a rare and inconsequential element in the Canadian economy. What it does mean is that there has been no systematic programme of nationalization. It has occurred and has been presented in case-by-case fashion.

Socialism has been attempted at the provincial level. In 1944, the CCF came to power in Saskatchewan and remained in power for twenty years. During that time, various socialist programmes were introduced. Before turning to the national scene, we will briefly review this provincial experience.

The most striking feature of Saskatchewan socialism was its agrarian base. Contrary to socialist theory, there was no appreciable industrial labour force or domestic capitalism. The CCF rose to power on a wave of populist-agrarian discontent common to the mid-western regions of North America.[1] The principal grievances arose out of the "cost-price squeeze" of the wheat farmers. There were wide fluctuations in grain prices, on the one hand, with the steadily rising costs of middleman, transport, machinery and borrowing costs on the other hand. The perceived enemies were the railroads, the manufacturers and the big banks – all with their headquarters in the East. This situation was enormously aggravated by the depression, which saw grain prices decline even faster than other prices.

Clearly, this was a promising situation for the politics of protest. Eventually the CCF realized this promise. However, both its coming to power and its behaviour in power were heavily conditioned by the non-socialist elements in the situation. The desperate farmers of Saskatchewan were not an industrial proletariat alienated and "amassed" in a Marxian sense. Their traditions were those of frontier or near-frontier settlers. In common with settlers everywhere, they deeply resented the urban establishment. Culturally they were individualistic and fundamentalist. There was considerable suspicion of intellectual socialism. For some it connoted Russia and atheism. The CCF reflected these traditions and accordingly played down doctrine and ideology.

Cultural conservatism was not the only defining characteristic of agrarian-socialism. The structure of the economy rested largely and rather precariously on a single activity – wheat growing. This qualified fundamentally any doctrine or programmes of public ownership. The idea of communal agriculture was anathema, and the industrial sector was virtually non-existent. The industrial or commercial infra-structure that existed was either small scale or else controlled from outside the province. Public ownership would either make little difference or run head on into national forces. The railroads and banks were subject to federal rather than provincial law. Further nationalization in these areas was subject to jurisdictional as well as political circumscription. Socialism in one agricultural province faced many limitations.

The CCF, despite ideological misgivings came to recognize and, indeed, to embody these limitations. A doctrine of private and public cooperation emerged. Provincial ownership was restricted to public utilities and natural resources, and then qualified with respect to the latter.

The one area where the doctrine of public ownership was applied was in the initiation and promotion (or salvaging) of high-risk enterprises. These have included such diverse and economically questionable activities as leather processing and box manufacturing. The results of this "state-entrepreneurship" have been sobering. Costs have been high, performance mediocre and the contribution to Saskatchewan's industrialization minimal.[2] As for the course of labour-relations, it would seem to illustrate the point made by British experience. Public ownership is no elixir for transforming managers and workers into soul mates.

Saskatchewan socialism was provincial and agrarian; hence, it was a peculiar (if not unusually peculiar) test of public ownership. To generalize from this case to Canada as a whole is a temptation often indulged but better resisted. There is available to us, furthermore, considerable Canadian experience with public-ownership, albeit of a non-doctrinaire variety. The difficult aspect of this experience – for the preachers of left and right – is that it leads to non-doctrinaire conclusions. Like many things Canadian, it is a mix and at times a muddle.

The first great federal "experiment" was the formation of the Canadian National Railways during World War I. It was an experiment very reluctantly undertaken only after the alternatives had been exhausted. There were two basic reasons for the decision. First, that a rail transport system was judged essential to the development of Canada. This was the "boom factor." Second, that by 1917 the system was threatened by the "melancholy progress of the Grand Trunk, Grand Trunk Pacific and Canadian Northern systems toward bankruptcy."[3] This was the "bust" factor. The government of the day had one compelling reason for not watching at a distance while the bust took place. It would have been busted too. Over a period of years, separate federal administrations had helped finance these rail lines. Bankruptcy would have seriously undermined the Canadian government's appeal to the money markets of the world.[4] And there were no private interests eagerly waiting to rescue the operation. The government was alone and responsible and it felt, by 1917, that "if the public does the financing, the public should enjoy the ultimate rewards".[5] Whether the public has enjoyed its rewards is another question.

Variations on the theme of "pragmatic nationalization"

have been played in the formation of other Crown Corporations. Polymer was formed as part of the war effort. Whether it was intended to remain a public corporation after the war is open to some debate. Trans Canada Airlines, now Air Canada, was formed with the rationale that Canadian competitiveness in this area required concentration of capital and coordination of efforts. There has been continuous and occasionally bitter controversy about this in Canada, as in other countries with national airlines. Since the war, concessions have been made to the privately owned Canadian Pacific Airlines, which has resulted in limited competition on domestic runs and a geographical division of bilateral franchises.

The Canadian Broadcasting Corporation was created in 1932 by a Conservative Government. Its justification was that "no other scheme than that of public ownership can ensure to the people of this country, without regard to class or place, equal enjoyment of the benefits and pleasure of radio broadcasting.[6] In the late 1950's permission was given by another Conservative Government for the formation of a private network. As a final example of Canadian nationalization, we might mention Atomic Energy of Canada Ltd, which was formed for reasons of strategic national interest.

These were some of the reasons for public ownership in Canada. They were always advanced cautiously and pragmatically. It was always made clear that nationalization was a reluctant necessity rather than an ideological imperative. One writer has suggested the following pattern:

For some reason private enterprise is found wanting. The usual condition where this occurs is the existence of some public need having common characteristics which private enterprise is unwilling to fill, should not be expected to fill or is unsuitable to fill.[7]

A trifle vague, perhaps, but the emphasis is right. C.D. Howe, the staunch defender of private enterprise who engineered the establishment of several Crown Corporations, stated that the only test of the strength and weakness of either private operation or government operation is what can best serve the needs of the public of Canada.[8] Howe had no doubts that private enterprise was the basic way to serve the public. When necessary, it could be supplemented by public enterprise.

If Canadian public ownership was a reluctant necessity, wisdom required that it conform as closely as possible to private ownership. There has been bi-partisan agreement on this, if not always on its implementation. Mackenzie King stated that the President of the CNR must have "precisely the same degree of latitude and freedom as the shareholders of the CP would give to Mr. Beatty" [CP President].[9] An early President of the CNR confirmed this piece of wisdom by declaring that "there is as much chance of politics getting into the CNR as there is of an elephant walking a tight rope."[10]

It has been suggested from time to time that the large creature had mastered the trick. There have been charges of partisan politics in the appointments and decisions of the CNR as well as of other Crown Corporations. As the British case makes clear, however, the issue of public ownership and control goes much deeper than this occasional hanky-panky. The question is what relationship policy does and should have to management? It is silly to imagine that the two can be entirely separated:

Politics involves policy, and if the cabinet is to remain responsible for policy an important sector of the economy run by a government corporation cannot be taken out of politics.[11]

It is equally silly to suppose that there is or can be a single pattern or rule in this relationship. The Crown Corporations and their services vary widely. Ministers and governments view the subject in different ways. General policy has been set down in the *Government Corporations Operation Act of 1946* and the *Financial Administration Act of 1951*. Both follow the common distinction between day-to-day operations, which are the responsibility of management, and general policy, which is the responsibility of government. But the enabling legislation of specific corporations differs greatly. At the one extreme is Polymer. Its board of directors is drawn almost exclusively from private industry, and it enjoys a very considerable measure of independence.[12] At the opposite extreme is the Central Mortgage and Housing Corporation. Three of the eight members of its board come from the Civil Service of Canada and its specific function is to administer the provisions of the National Housing Act.[13]

While the law sets certain broad limits for the operation of these corporations, this is not the whole story by a long shot. Take the case of CMHC. When the Task Force on Housing and Urban Development was examining the relationship between the law and the practices of the Corporation, it could not find a single general policy directive or "set of principles" sent to the Corporation in its twenty-year history. That did not mean, however, that influence was not flowing. I have mentioned in another context the action of Robert Winters ordering CMHC to remove the fixed selling prices of housing. On a day-to-day basis there is a tremendous amount of two-way pressure between the government and the Corporation. There is pressure to make loans to specific companies, to make loans to specific places and on occasion to make special arrangements. Into the category of "arrangements" falls a situation in Windsor a few years ago. Striking Ford workers brought pressure to bear on the local M.P. to have mortgage payments deferred. CMHC complied. The more government becomes involved in home financing the more likely are such arrangements. Pressure groups form, become aware of their own political influence, and governments react.

CMHC is not an isolated case. Other examples of such day-to-day influence readily come to mind. The decision by CNR to continue extensive passenger service was, from an economic standpoint, a basic error. Management tried to buck the trends but failed. Losses ran as high as $75 million a year. Belated attempts to change the policy have been frustrated by continuous political pressure applied to the CNR. The problem is that people expect more from institutions they own even when they are losing money because the service is largely unused. CPR has had far less difficulty in reacting to the economic facts of life caused by changing technology.

One of the most striking illustrations of the fact that politics and management do not mix well was Air Canada's decision to move a maintenance base from Winnipeg to Montreal. During the 1962 election campaign, Mr. Pearson made a speech in Winnipeg saying that the base would remain for some time. The general information on which the speech was based had been checked with Air Canada management in advance. Subsequently, the airline executive changed its mind on the timing. The transfer was to take place sooner than announced. All hell broke loose in Winnipeg. Groups and more groups and countergroups formed. The Manitoba government entered the fray. So did the machinists' union. Names were called and charges were made. The affair even managed to generate its quota of Canadian racism – Winnipeg *vs.* Montreal.

When I came along, I had the unhappy job of trying to unravel the whole thing. It was one of the most troublesome problems that faced me as Minister of Transport. We finally reached a compromise settlement but only after much bitterness and more noise. Whether the decision to move the base was correct or not, I do not know. It probably was, although I never had complete confidence in the information supplied by the airline. If the airline had not been publicly owned, however, the issue would not have been raised as it was and the debate would not have been so prolonged.

Air Canada has had other problems in managing its facilities. On one occasion it was "ordered" to extend service to Muskoka Airport. The order probably came by way of a suggestion on the "old boy net." Action was initiated by the powerful C.D. Howe, at the urging of Bucko MacDonald, M.P. for Parry Sound. Bucko was a fine hockey player. He was also fine at representing his constituents. The air service made Bucko a hero but, unfortunately, that was all it made. It lost money and the service was soon discontinued.

Let me cite one other example of unfortunate political interference in the management of Crown Corporations. This is the famous – or infamous – Seaway settlement of 1966. After negotiations had broken down and a strike loomed, the federal government appointed a mediator. He proceeded to recommend an incredible wage increase, about 30 per cent over two years. The government – despite the profound objections of the Seaway Authority management – accepted the recommendation. In my view this was one of the worst economic mistakes ever made in this country. It was a landmark in the wage-price spiral of the past few years.

What is the point of all these examples? Only that where

public corporations are in direct contact with the public there will be political intervention on a day-to-day basis. It is idle to blame politics for this. It is the principal business of politics to represent public demand. But it is not necessarily wise to facilitate the direct intervention of the public in economic decision-making based on emotion rather than reason.

The commercially successful Crown Corporations illustrate the point. Polymer is comparatively independent of politics. The general public – and the general politician – know it only by name. The Corporation is regarded as extremely well run. It has good management and it shows good results. Polymer thrives in relative obscurity. The same could be said of *Canadian Overseas Telecommunications Corporation*. As Minister of Transport, my main contact with management was the presentation of the annual report, which showed an excellent profit. Because the company does not affect many Canadians in their daily lives, very few are aware of its existence.

The possible dangers of substituting political for economic decisions are perhaps best illustrated in the case of Deuterium Canada Ltd. The Glace Bay heavy water plant is the white elephant of the nuclear world. Its costs have risen enormously and it remains many months, perhaps years, from operation. As in all such cases, there is a complex variety of reasons for failure. One basic factor, however, was the political decision to locate the plant in Glace Bay in the first place. The decision ignored sound economic reasons for locating in Whiteshell, Manitoba and contracting with General Electric of Canada. The cost of the decision – now running into the tens of millions of dollars – is, of course, borne by the Canadian taxpayer.

Political decisions are not necessarily uneconomic or irrational. When properly developed and scrutinized, they may serve vital national interests and encourage economic development. But there is often a haphazard or "special interest" element in politics that may interfere with sound business operation. The activities of parliament illustrate this. The question period rarely sheds much light on the Crown Corporations. The Committee system has not performed much better. Examination of accounts tends to be superficial and inconstant. Of course, the quality varies with the preparedness of Committee Members but there are major difficulties. A Chairman of the

Public Accounts Committee has commented: "If we were to sit 24 hours a day, six days a week, here in this committee room from now to the end of the session, we could not go over all these companies."[14]

My own conclusion is that there is seldom any intrinsic merit in public ownership. Companies that do not affect the public directly can be equally well run as nationalized or private enterprises.[15] Companies that affect peoples' lives directly on a day-to-day basis will, invariably, be subject to a greater degree of irrationality if publicly owned. There is, consequently, no advantage to nationalization except in cases where private initiative is unable or unwilling to provide the desired good or service. These cases will be the exception, rather than the rule.

The dream of a "perfect" public ownership is just that, a dream. It offers its adherents the opportunity to escape from the imperfect world of reality to the "utopian ideal" of make believe.

Notes

1. An excellent general study of the origins of agrarian-socialism is Seymour Martin Lipset, *Agrarian Socialism: The Cooperative Commonwealth Federation in Saskatchewan. A Study in Political Sociology*, (New York: Anchor Books, 1968).

2. The "great debate" on these experiments took place at Mossbank, Saskatchewan in May 1957 between Premier T.C. Douglas and a disillusioned renegade from the CCF, Ross Thatcher. The outcome of the debate was itself debated but the critic of public ownership did sufficiently well to propel him down the road to becoming Liberal Premier of Saskatchewan. For an account of the debate see Robert Tyre, *Douglas in Saskatchewan: The Story of a Socialist Experiment*, (Vancouver: Mitchell Press, 1962), Chapter Six, "Debate at Mossbank," pp. 94-125. This is generally considered to be a strongly biased account, but interesting, nevertheless.

3. G.R. Stevens, *Canadian National Railways*, Vol. II, (Toronto: Clarke, Irwin & Co. Ltd., 1962), p. 455.

4. *Ibid.*, Chap. 17, "Political Background to a Merger."

5. Lloyd D. Musolf, *Public Ownership and Accountability: The Canadian Experience*, (Cambridge: Harvard University Press, 1959), p. 9. There is nothing like the volume or quality of literature on Canadian public ownership that exists in Great Britain. This reflects not only the more modest resources of Canadian scholarship but also the "non-ideological" nature of the Canadian experience. None of the existing literature makes a serious attempt to assess the performance of the Crown Corporations. Any conclusions must be tentative.

6. Statement by Prime Minister Bennett quoted in C.A. Ashley and R.G.H. Smails, *Canadian Crown Corporations: Some Aspects of their Administration and Control*, (Toronto: Macmillan Company of Canada, Ltd., 1965), p. 130.
7. Ashley and Smails, *Canadian Crown Corporations*, p. 7.
8. Statement quoted in Musolf, *Public Ownership and Accountability*, p. 25.
9. Statement quoted, *Ibid.*, p. 21.
10. Statement quoted in Ashley and Smails, *Canadian Crown Corporations*, p. 9.
11. J.E. Hodgetts, *Proceedings of the Fifth Annual Conference of the Institute of Public Ownership of Canada* quoted in Ashley and Smails, *Canadian Crown Corporations*, p. 9.
12. R.W. Todgham, a director of Polymer, observed in 1961: "An important contribution to Polymer's success has been the freedom from what I myself call political pressures," quoted in Ashley and Smails, *Canadian Crown Corporations*, pp. 250-51.
13. Ashley and Smails, *Canadian Crown Corporations*, p. 76-77.
14. Quoted *Ibid.*, pp. 76-77.
15. Assumes management of equal calibre in both cases.

Chapter **8**

The Soviet Union: Socialist Promise and Performance in One Country

The theory behind the Socialist revolution, as Lenin made clear in his *State and Revolution,* included the withering away of the state once the proletarian revolution was complete and the new order established. He was at pains to clear up a commonly-held misconception that the new order could evolve through all its stages from bourgeois capitalism to Utopia – a heresy he considered "opportunism." He stated that the bourgeois state is ended by the proletariat in the course of the revolution.[1] He also explained that only in a communist society, where capitalism has completely disappeared and there are no classes, is it possible to speak of freedom. Only when the people are "freed from capitalist slavery" will they discover the "elementary rules of social life" and be able to observe them without the compulsion of the state.[2]

Presumably, too, once the ownership of the tools of production were transferred to the proletariat, the efficiency of production would improve to the point where the physical needs of all would be met on a scale hitherto unknown. All that was required was an end to the ruthless exploitation of labour by the capitalists.

After half a century, it is fair to take stock of the achievement of the great experiment in collective ownership and to observe the extent of practical success. Space will only permit a few brief observations and examples.[3]

One of the fundamental errors of the new order was the collectivization of agriculture. Of course, it was part of the utopian philosophy and had to be implemented, but it did not work. The fierce resistance of the peasants and the bloody purge necessary to force collectivization were grotesque reminders that the revolution lacked the widespread support of the people whose lives were most directly affected. Western assessments of fragmentary statistical information indicate that during the period 1928-1932, when forced collectivization was underway, there was a substantial fall in per capita consumption with real wages dropping by perhaps as much as 40 per cent. Per capita output of the really critical food product, grain, fell by something like 10 per cent while per capita output of meat, milk and eggs was down by 47, 37 and 61 per cent respectively. There is evidence that these shortages, plus what appear to have been punitive measures in important grain growing areas (Ukraine), caused grave suffering.

Even today there are many shortages. Soviet gold reserves have been depleted to finance wheat contracts. Much of the beef which has been and is now available comes from animals raised for general purposes by farmers with little incentive to improve the quality of their stock. Prices of meat are high, and steak, chops and roasts are virtually unavailable. Fresh fruit is a luxury for most Soviet citizens.

The only possible explanation for this chronic shortage is the collective system. Where collective farmers have a small plot of land under their own control, they produce. These tiny plots of privately-controlled land provide much of the fresh produce for Moscow. Without them, the supply situation would be chaotic.

The lack of incentive on the collective farms is easy to sense. One farmer told me he makes 90 rubles a month as manager of a 500 cowherd. His pay would go up to 110 rubles a month if he increased milk production by 20 per cent. "But," he asked, "what's the use?" So little merchandise reaches his village that he cannot spend his present salary. In fact, he was so flush with rubles that he wanted to pay for breakfast. His wife gets 60 rubles a month for picking fruit. Hardly a king's ransom, but enough to live on. The farm offered few modern luxuries. There was no inside plumbing, for example, and the communal bath was available just once a week for each group. But there was a certain philosophical resignation toward life, conditioned perhaps by the knowledge that escape was impossible.

Soviet industry, too, is hamstrung by too much centralized control and decision making. The complexity of modern economic systems involves millions of individual decisions. There is no effective way that a centralized planning agency or group of agencies can make all of these decisions. A few paragraphs from *Workers Paradise Lost* give the gist of the problem:

"First there is the universal practice by factory managements of fabricating their own secondary supplies, because they dare not trust other sources to make deliveries at the proper time or of the proper kinds. To fulfill plans, 'Soviet factories tend to grow into highly integrated empires which, instead of getting their semi-manufactured products, such as castings, forgings, spare parts, from large-scale, efficient, specialized outside suppliers, produce them in their own plants, on an uneconomically small scale . . . at a prohibitive cost.'

"Every factory thus is likely to maintain a series of auxiliaries. It costs ten to twenty times as much, for example, to produce screws and nuts on a tiny scale than in big specialized plants. But what is cost when the plan itself is at stake? Practically all machine tool factories have their own forge shops, whereas in the United States only fourteen in a thousand have them.

"Second, along with the industrial "giants" there are large numbers of small, outmoded units. In the Russian republic alone, supplementing the dozens of huge modern rolling mills, there are in operation eighty small ones, dating from the nineteenth and even the eighteenth century. There productivity per worker is fantastically low, but in its anxiety for plan fulfillment, the trust dares not close down even the smallest and most inefficient operation under its control.

*"The same holds true for other trusts. In the electric in-
dustry, the planner focused on large, district stations and their
output has steadily increased. At the same time, there are
53,000 pygmy stations with average capacity of 50 kilowatts,
maintained and added to despite the fact that their power costs
ten to twenty times more.*

*"Eighteenth-century steel mills and 50-kilowatt stations",
Dr. Smolinski attests, "continued to crowd the path of Soviet
industrialization and lower the overall efficiency with which
Soviet industry operates". He does not add, because it is implicit, that in a competitive economy, the uneconomical an-
tiques would have been driven out of existence."[4]*

The blind pursuit of production goals in terms of aggregates is not only inefficient, but is also responsible for some
enormous sacrifices of quality and variety. One of the most
common complaints levelled at Russian manufactures is the
poor quality and monotonous lack of imagination. If the incentive for factory managers and workers is related to output,
without qualifications in respect of quality or marketability, the
result is inevitable. Drabness, shoddiness and uniformity are not
only predictable, but profitable for the producer, if not for
society at large. Without a genuine system of costing and the
discipline of the market, a significant amount of production is
useless as many chock-a-block warehouses will attest.

A brilliant Yugoslav economist, in explaining why production in Yugoslavia had risen so fast in one year, stated
candidly that they had produced many unwanted items. It was
a mistake, he explained, which had not been repeated the
following year when production, though increasing more slowly,
was related more directly to popular demand.

The Soviets, unlike the Yugoslavs, do not admit mistakes.
Consequently there would appear to be no reason to change
their system but for the fact that it cannot match well-managed
competitive systems. Soviet economic performance with respect
to medium term planning targets has not been uniformly bad.
The 1965 targets set out in the 1959-1965 Seven Year Plan
for economic aggregates such as national income and gross
industrial production were, in the first case, only slightly below
expectation and, in the second case, slightly above expectation.

Raw material and commodity targets such as those for iron ore, pig iron, steel, oil and electricity were fulfilled. The grain target was not fulfilled, however, nor were the targets for meat, gas, mineral fertilizer and leather footwear. The boast by Premier Khrushchev, in the early 1960's, that by the end of the decade the Soviet Union would have the world's highest living standard and outstrip the United States in total industrial production was considerably off the mark.

The specific production targets for 1970 are in all cases lower than the goals proclaimed publicly by Khrushchev at the Party Congress in 1961. Steel production estimated to be 126 million tons in 1970 is about 22 per cent less than the 160 million tons Khrushchev had predicted. Oil was to reach 429 million tons; it has come reasonably close at 385. By contrast, gas production is about a third below the 1961 forecast. Fertilizers are 25 per cent below the targeted figure.

The same trend holds in the area of consumer goods and food. Shoe production in 1970 fell some 200 million pairs short of Khrushchev's hopes. Far more important is that the present grain quotas (194 million tons) are significantly below the planning objective (260 million tons).

Although production has increased substantially in the decade, all the evidence suggests that growth has been very modest when compared with official proclamations. The combination of capital formation, labour productivity and technological advance is not sufficient to support extraordinary growth. Present plans are more modest and there is no indication that an attempt will be made to recoup the 1970 shortfall.

When Dmitri Poliansky was touring the wheat plains of Western Canada, he inquired as to where the houses of the peasants were located. Informed that there were no peasants and that the farmer, his wife and family were themselves the operators, he was at first incredulous. He then asked why the farmer was not working. "It is Saturday afternoon and the farmer and his family have gone to town." "Is it a national holiday?" Mr. Poliansky responded. "No, it is customary for farmers who usually complete their work during the week to take Saturday afternoon off." The visitor was impressed. Anyone who has seen the large clusters of houses in collectivized villages would understand why. There is an enormous contrast between these overstaffed and under-industrialized Soviet experiments and the highly-capitalized and incredibly efficient North American farms.

The Soviet leaders have long realized that their subjects are not sufficiently "evolved" so as to produce according to their abilities. Even the scale of extra rewards and special penalties has been judged inadequate. The new labour code provides penalties in housing and other areas for workers who do not perform their jobs properly. According to V.I. Prokhorov, Secretary of the Central Council of Trade Unions, this law is the first real consolidation of the "carrot and stick" rules. The article of the new law which deals with disciplinary measures against workers only mentions the traditional ones such as rebuke, dismissal, demotion or trial by a comrades' court. But the preceding article concerning housing, holiday trips and other privileges indicated that priority will be given to workers "who successfully and conscientiously fulfill their labour obligations."

This measure gives the authorities considerable power to reward or punish, as the case may be, those who meet or fall short of the production goals set for them. In particular, the acute housing shortage in the Soviet Union provides considerable power over those workers desperately in need of accommodation. The state owns and directly allocates some two-thirds of the total urban housing stock, and is also the principal builder of new housing, accounting for about four-fifths of the total in 1968. The waiting lists for new apartments are still long; eighteen months to three years is typical in most cities. The threat of being dropped a year or two on the waiting list could be a significant influence in determining work habits.

The kind of power available under this law is just one more reminder that the dictatorship is not one of the proletariat, but of the ruling elite. The state has not withered away. As a matter of fact, the process has not even begun after a fifty-three year incubation period. Nor will it.

The ruling class is a privileged class. It has many of the privileges and perquisites that the proletariat are still struggling for. They have housing accommodation on a scale commensurate with their responsibility and position in the hierarchy. They have good food, both domestic and imported. Special lists are maintained at cinemas for people who do not have to stand in the queue. They have the good life and are determined to maintain it in the only way possible in a somewhat hostile environment — by maintaining absolute control.

The scale of privilege can be gauged by looking at the income distribution. An average Russian may earn 110-120 rubles a month; an engineer 165-195, depending on experience. He can increase this by 10 per cent if he speaks one of the Western languages in addition to Russian, for example, French, English or German. A working knowledge of an Eastern language such as Japanese rates a 20 per cent bonus. A taxi driver's salary would be approximately 110 rubles per month, a sweeper's, 70, a farm foreman's, 90, and his working wife's, 60 per month. In contrast, a three-star general receives 800-900 rubles a month, plus the maximum in perquisites. A conscript doing his stint for the motherland gets 3 rubles each month.

Even without putting a money value on the perquisites, the difference between the incomes of a three-star general and an ordinary worker is far greater in the USSR than in Canada or the United States. Including those "special" rewards, the difference would be several times greater than in North America. So much for the classless society!

Another revolutionary promise was Lenin's pledge that all groups would enjoy the democratic freedoms, including the right of self-determination. Eugene Lyons describes it this way:

> *The central promises were explicit in Lenin's pre-Revolutionary writings. He demanded unrestricted mobility for the peasant, release of all political prisoners, severe punishment for officials who made arbitrary arrests or imprisoned anyone without trial. 'Until freedom of assembly, of speech and the press is declared' he said, 'there would be persecution of 'unofficial faith, unofficial opinion, unofficial doctrines'.*[5]

He insisted on the elimination of the death penalty and of the internal passport.

In the months before the October coup, the Bolshevik press and speeches recapitulated these pledges and added more for good measure. The Soviets, when entrusted with all power, would be "fully democratic," allowing peaceful struggle among all non-bourgeois parties. They would assure "genuine freedom of the press for all." All the nationalities in the country would enjoy self-determination; in Lenin's words, "full restitution of freedom to Finland, the Ukraine, White Russia, the Moslems, etc., . . . including even freedom to secede."

Refugees from the Baltic countries, the Ukraine, and other minority regions must go into hysterics when they read that bit of prophetic Leninism. Undeniably, certain forms of cultural expression by the nationalities are allowed and even encouraged. But what is not allowed is any form of cultural expression that would threaten the unity of the Soviet state. Various kinds of administrative pressure are used to ensure that expressions of national culture are confined in practice to a certain limited use of language rights and to cultural manifestations roughly at the level of folklore.

Anyone who wants a sophisticated technical or professional education pretty well has to get it in Russian, and the higher forms of cultural expression, while heavily dependent on non-Russian talent, are really a part of Russian culture. Russification proceeds at a pace consistent with the avoidance of open rebellion. At the same time, nationalism simmers just beneath the surface and manifests itself in various ways such as refusal to use the Russian language in the classroom. Hundreds of Ukranian intellectuals have been harassed for conduct as inoffensive as possession of non-Soviet books about the history of the Ukraine. Some who have been bold enough to put their feelings on paper have been sentenced and confined in Soviet labour camps.

Jews have been subject to rigorous oppression. Only a trickle of Jewish emigration to Israel has actually been allowed, even in the period since 1967. They are "discouraged" from maintaining their religious identity. There are no Jewish schools. In Moscow, where there are more than a quarter of a million Jews, there are only two synagogues. There are no Jewish newspapers and only one magazine, which faithfully adheres to the "party line." Whether from fear that Jews will put Israel ahead of their Soviet homeland at a time when the Kremlin is playing a game of "russian roulette" power politics in the Middle East, or from suspicion that the intellectual curiosity of the Jews will encourage them to challenge the status quo, the fact is that these people have been subjected to special and harsh attention.

This fear of ethnic and cultural minorities within the

frontiers of the Union has its external counterpart in the balance of the Soviet Empire – the Warsaw Block. Russian troops marched in and crushed the revolt of East German workers when they rebelled against their communist government in 1953. Hungarian rebels were suppressed by Soviet tanks during their uprising against their Red Masters in 1956. The Dubcek government of Czechoslovakia was overthrown by the intervention of the Soviet army when it attempted to take an independent, though still communist, road in 1968. Getting too far out of line is not tolerated – even in the Empire.

In summary, the dream is dead. Lenin's vision was a "dictatorship of the proletariat." The reality is a dictatorship of the party élite. Together with other socialist intellectuals, he dreamed of a "withering away" of the State as forecast by Marx, his mentor. In reality a huge top-heavy bureaucracy of aged "conservatives" rules the land and manages the property with an iron hand. The dream was a classless society. The reality is a ruling class more privileged and stratified than that of any western democracy. The dream included great wealth and a more efficient productive capability than that of the decadent bourgeois democracies. The reality is the same relative position among industrialized countries as fifty years ago.

Students of comparative systems should thoughtfully reflect on the stark contrast between the hopes and promises of 1917 and the reality of 1970 – the pre-revolutionary assurances and the post-revolutionary performance.

Notes

1. Lenin, *State and Revolution*, (New York: International Publishers, 1969), p. 171.
2. *Ibid.*
3. For a critical review by an outsider, one might read *Workers Paradise Lost*, by Eugene Lyons. (© 1967 by Eugene Lyons. Reprinted with permission of the publisher, Funk & Wagnall's) For a moving account of the tragedies of Soviet Communism, by one deeply devoted to Russia, read *The First Circle,* by Alexander Solzhenitsyn, (New York: Harper and Row Publishers, Inc., 1968).
4. Eugene Lyons, *Workers Paradise Lost*, © 1967 by Eugene Lyons. Reprinted with permission of the publisher, Funk & Wagnall's, pp. 166-67.
5. *Ibid.*

Chapter **9**

The Soviet Union:
The State Church

Of all the objections to the Soviet system and there are many including the drabness, the monotony, the economic inefficiency and its consequent hardship, the one that for me is conclusive is the tyranny of the State church, communism. My hostility to this is unbounded and can best be described by a comment made by Thomas Jefferson at the time of the presidential campaign of 1800. The clergy, convinced that under the Jeffersonians their influence would decline, were particularly virulent in their opposition. In a letter to Dr. Benjamin Rush, Jefferson wrote: "And they believe rightly; for I have sworn upon the altar of God, eternal hostility toward every form of tyranny over the mind of man."[1]

The philosopher, Alfred North Whitehead,[2] has described the gradual movement "from force to persuasion" as one of the central developments of our civilization. Certainly Whitehead knew when he wrote those words that this was a tragically incomplete development, and the past few decades have raised the deepest doubts as to whether we have progressed at all. We have made some progress in the social field. Much of the extreme

74

exploitation and human degradation that affected Marx so deeply has been eliminated in those parts of the world that concerned him most. On the other hand, those conditions remain in some parts of the world and the evidence of man's continuing urge to violence and his mania for intolerance is enormous.

Communism is not the only faith that has justified the terrorizing and persecution of men in our times. Nor are these ideological habits an invention of communism. Christianity has at times made enormous contributions to this anti-tradition of our civilization. To recognize this we need only recall the familiar story of the Universal Church and the Reformation of the late middle ages. This was the Great Age of Faith. It was also a great age of violence and persecution.

The man of that time always oscillated between the fear of hell and the most naïve joy, between cruelty and tenderness, between harsh asceticism and insane attachment to the delights of this world, between hatred and goodness . . .[3]

It would be some defence of Christianity to say that these hatreds existed despite the faith, that they were manifestations of a worldliness and selfishness that the Church could not control. In some cases this was so. The Church did produce men like St. Francis. But it was also the case that an important part of the hatred and violence and persecution radiated from the faith itself. Christianity was not only a loving creed. It was also a passionately fearful and hating creed. Holiness had a deadly air about it.

The logic of the Christian fear – so familiar to us that it appears banal – is perhaps best illustrated by the dilemma of an abbot during one of the Crusades. He was faced with the problem of differentiating true believers from heretics.

"What shall we do Lord? We cannot discern between the good and the evil." The Abbot (fearing, as also did the rest, lest they, the heretics, should feign themselves Catholics from fear of death, and should return again to their faithlessness after his departure) is said to have answered: "Slay them, for God knoweth his own." So there they were slain in countless multitudes in that city.[4]

The pious may prefer to think that this familiar motto

"When in doubt kill" was a rare exception. In fact it was not. Many of the reform movements in Catholicism were charged with a wish to eradicate and destroy rather than to unite and heal. Pope Innocent III bound Christian rulers, upon threat of excommunication, "to exterminate from the lands subject to their obedience all heretics who have been marked out by the Church."[5] Pope Nicholas V authorized the enslavement of the Moors. The common element in these actions was fear of the creeping, insidious influence of the heathen and the heretic, the outsider and the doubter.

It is one of the myths of our history to imagine that the Reformation was a glorious rebellion against this spirit of intolerance, that protestantism stood for freedom of conscience and mind. Nothing could be further from the truth. While the long-range consequences of splitting the faith may have been to allow tolerance and intellectual dissent some leeway, this was by no means the intention or the spirit of the protestant leaders.

Martin Luther began his rebellion with a cry for the primacy of conscience. Having acquired power, however, he revealed that it was his conscience he had in mind and not conscience in general. He damned theological speculation with the words "Dame Reason, that silly little fool, that whore, that Devil's bride." He observed of the people "The brute populace must be governed by brute force. I would rather suffer a Prince doing wrong than a people doing right." And most tragic of all he supplied a generation of Nazis with chapter and verse of the most vile anti-semitism.

In this regard, Luther was not a deviant protestant. John Calvin's Geneva was a model of administrative intolerance and conformity. It revealed a genius for regulating the minutiae of faith. And it was a genius capable of murder. When the Spanish heretic, Servetus, made the mistake of passing through Geneva he was ordered arrested by Calvin and was promptly hurried on his way to eternity via the stake. Protestant leaders everywhere joined Melanchton in praising this "signal act of piety."

This kind of cruel nonsense has long since passed. Admittedly there are some embarrassing remnants of intolerance like the unconscionable display of a few militants in the Irish North. But these are exceptions to the general rule. For the most part, Christianity has become tame and tolerant.

It is ironic that paralleling this most welcome moderation on the part of practicing Christians a new religion should be born to resurrect, perpetuate and intensify the religious oppression of ages past. Communism, described by some as the wave of the future, has been the spiritual fountainhead of terror, oppression, coercion and intolerance. The crimes perpetrated and being perpetrated by this new religion make the historical precedents appear pale by comparison. Its bloody purges represent a new order of magnitude in mass murder. It is the State Church of Russia and its Imperialistic Empire, the Union of Soviet Socialist Republics.

Learning from the experience of others, the leaders of the new Communist church know the value of early indoctrination. It is one of the useful by-products of supervised play and instruction of children of working mothers. Children are taught "right-thinking" by qualified teachers. The uniformed "Young Pioneers" are a special elite of Soviet youth. Patterned to a certain extent after the Boy Scout movement, the organization provides a careful blend of physical, social and intellectual (spiritual) instruction.

Having been exposed to the "catechism" at a tender age, the Young Pioneers are well qualified for graduation to the Komsomol where similar but more advanced activities and instruction can be pursued to the age of majority. The Komsomol is the Communist youth group. It has characteristics in common with other religious youth groups and its members represent an elite of Soviet youth. Ambitious young people and the children of ambitious parents are well aware of the significant advantages that accrue in later life to those with well-documented records of achievement in the Komsomol. It is "good" to be in the good books of "the church." The advantages, as has been pointed out, are tangible as well as spiritual and it may be that some youngsters are more influenced by the former than by the latter.

The Komsomol is a good training ground for entry into the religious hierarchy. Local party bosses, district party bosses, city party bosses, all officials up to and including the Council of Ministers and the head of State must be members of "the Church" in good standing. Only loyal communists need apply and early association and "baptism" must inevitably be part of the screening process. The clever, the calculating, the devout and the inspired then compete to make their way up the ladder of achievement to more responsible positions in the "religious hierarchy." The "Church" has its "Bishops" and its "Archbishops," the coveted senior posts of party power and privilege.

The privileges of clergy are traditional. The "Priests" and "Primates" of the new communist "Church" maintain the tradition brilliantly. Party members have many perquisites and privileges. Special rest homes and vacation centres are available at choice resort areas such as the Black Sea. More senior members of the hierarchy have summer homes, *dachas*, where they can retreat from the tensions of urban life. Some high government officials live in stately single family dwellings, a rare luxury in this era of prefabricated, precast, high-rise concrete boxes. There are special stores available to party members where imported and luxury items, not available to the lowly "parishioners" at any price, may be purchased. From quality meats seldom seen by ordinary citizens to chauffeur-driven cars, one can observe the broad range of privileges available to the "spiritual" leaders and temporal masters of Soviet society. They have much to protect.

To remind the masses of the improvement of their situation, a number of new "churches" have been built. Probably the most impressive of these is the Exhibition of Economic Achievement on the outskirts of Moscow. There, to the stirring sounds of martial music, one may watch a variety of films or observe one of a multitude of exhibits demonstrating the dramatic achievements of the post-revolutionary period. Faith without good works is dead. Therefore, myriad statistics proclaim the miraculous works made possible by the faith. In 1913, there were 1.8 doctors per 10,000 population. Today this ratio is much more favorable, surpassing the United States by one-third, though no mention is made of the continuing shortage of hospitals or up-to-date hospital equipment. The income of collective farmers has increased by 31 per cent from 1965-1968. Again there is no mention that this income, although enough to live on, may be of limited value due to the critical shortage of consumer goods in the villages. There are regulations that prohibit farmers from leaving their farms and going to the cities without permission; however, leakage of manpower from farm labour to industrial labour groups has been a fairly constant feature of the labour scene for some time. In fifty years, 2.3 billion square meters of housing was built and from 1966-69, 44 million people got new flats. These are impressive figures. But no mention is made of the poor finish in the prefabricated flats or of the long waiting periods. The "Church" emphasizes the positive aspects of Soviet achievement, not the negative. This is a normal "religious" habit. The tragedy exists in the absence of spiritual competition.

Nearby, stretching its graceful head toward the stars, is one of the new idols, the Monument to the Space Explorers. The graceful lines and slim profile silhouette its stark beauty against the afternoon sky. How fitting that it should reach so far toward heaven, and so dramatically. Have the spacemen sought God in the course of extraterrestrial journeys? Have they sought in vain? Perhaps they have found "Him" at the very gates of the Kremlin.

It seems that every religion, even one allegedly based on scientific materialism, must have some generally recognized God. Soviet Communism, being no exception, has deified Lenin. The 100th anniversary of Lenin's birth gave new impetus to a process already begun. Placards, banners, statues, buttons and badges, full face and profile, Lenin was everywhere. In bronze and brass and iron, in paper, plaster, plastic and Neon lights, Lenin was everywhere. In apartment, store, subway, restaurant and opera, Lenin was everywhere.

Most incredible of all were the earthly remains. The truncated tattooed body of the man himself, testing a kind of material immortality through the grace of a pump circulating embalming fluid constantly through veins, is lying perpetually in state. The devout, the sincere, the cynical and the curious form a queue a mile long and eight abreast just to catch a fleeting glimpse of the immortal revolutionary.

Above the streets, banners proclaim "Lenin Lived, Lives and Will Live" and "Time has no power over Lenin. He is as Eternal as Life Itself". This Leninania must be the most persistent and expensive posthumous deification in history.

Simultaneous with this revolutionary idolatry is the systematic repression of religious competition. The struggle to stamp out Christianity in the Soviet Union has been widely reported. It is still a live issue. The policy being pursued has been designed to "strike at any living religious institution and favour those which show a weakening of the spirit." In 1969, a breakaway group of Baptists who left the Evangelical Christian Baptist Church because of the latter's subservience to the regime became the object of government displeasure. The Russian Orthodox Church has bought, at a very high price, its survival and the Kremlin protection of its establishment.[6] That price is represented in the words of *The Journal of Moscow Patriarchate*, "The cause of the revolution is the cause of the Orthodox Church." As might be expected, outspoken critics of this alliance are subject to repression. The existence on paper of the Orthodox Church and its foreign relations are a useful adjunct to the foreign relations of the Communist Party.

Like Christians in the days of the Crusades and the Inquisition, faithful communists (or socialists, as many of them prefer to be called) believe that their religion is not only superior, but the only "true" religion. This is always a dangerous assumption especially when one believes that the "true" religion is so advantageous and essential for all men that it must be universally accepted even if this means "crushing the skulls of infidels." The first step in this procedure, of course, is to dispatch from the mother church missionaries who will carry the gospel to the ends of the earth. The missionaries establish their "cells" of intimates and these, in turn, establish new cells which extend their influence into positions of power and influence in order to "take the gospel unto every creature."

Some insight into the "missionary" system in Canada was provided in 1945, by the Soviet cypher clerk, Igor Gouzenko. In defecting to Canada, Gouzenko brought with him from the Soviet Embassy certain documents which implicated a number of Canadians in espionage activities. The first reaction of the Canadian Prime Minister, MacKenzie King, was characteristic. He was incredulous and concerned about the possible effects on Canadian-Soviet relations. He doubted that Stalin, his recent ally, would knowingly condone such activity. Later when he finally appreciated the enormity of the network, his attitude changed sharply.

It is possible that these influences have continued in an extensive way. Certainly as a member of the Cabinet Committee on Security, I was impressed by Royal Canadian Mounted

Police estimates of the number of active missionaries. This was especially disturbing in the case of certain movements such as Quebec separatism. Here it would seem there has been a very distinct, if peripheral, influence at work.

I have long felt the importance in a democratic society of establishing and disclosing such influence as clearly as possible. I am aware of the difficulty of doing this. McCarthyism was a vile and hysterical reaction to this problem. There must be no witchhunts. It is, however, the responsibility of society to discover and reveal the kinds and degrees of influence within itself. There are unconscious social and political motivations. There are people participating in actions, the end result of which they would oppose if they understood. The possibilities of establishing open and fair procedures whereby these things can be rationally discussed concerns me deeply. There is far too much public ignorance and, thus, public irrationality in these matters.

The "mother church" and its hierarchy, in order to sustain itself in power, has been forced to resort to brutal oppression at home. Stalin, described by former Yugoslav communist Vice-President Milovan Djilas as "the greatest criminal in history," may have executed or starved as many as 20 million of his own people. He boasted of 10 million killed during the forced collectivization of farms. The history of mass murder and bloody tyranny is well known and there is no point in repeating it here. For those who think that repression has ended and a new day of liberalization begun, it may be useful to refer to one or two recent dispatches. It is true that the punishments are not as severe as in the Stalin era and more printed heresy does appear. The line between what is acceptable and what is not still exists, however, and those who cross it either deliberately or inadvertently soon know at first hand the total power of the State apparatus and the dreaded secret police.

Sviatoslav Karavanskyi, a fifty-year-old Ukrainian journalist, was arrested in 1969 and sentenced to thirty years at hard labour for "anti-Soviet activities" soon after his release from captivity after serving twenty years at hard labour for the same charge.

An Associated Press dispatch from Prague published in the Toronto Daily Star on Friday, January 16, 1970, read in part as follows:

"Czech police have arrested 1,740 people in a round-up of "criminal elements," Prague Radio said last night. The radio said checks were made on more than 18,000 people during surprise raids on 2,502 places in Bohemia and Moravia Wednesday night. In Prague, 300 persons were detained and 112 of them were jailed."

Another AP report from Moscow stated:

"Mass arrests by Soviet secret police and trials reminiscent of the Stalin era were reported yesterday by Soviet dissidents. Some feared it was "the beginning of a widespread purge." In the biggest single arrest, 160 Tartars were reported rounded up by KGB plainclothesmen in Moscow during last week's Lenin centennial celebrations when they arrived to demonstrate in front of the Lenin Library for the return of their Crimean homeland and restoration of the civil rights they lost in World War II."

The "democratization," as some Western observers refer to the change in Soviet practice, is more apparent than real. Although some forms of dissent are not suppressed as automatically, ruthlessly and completely as in the Stalin era, this is more a reflection of the degree to which the Kremlin has consolidated its power than of anything else. Dissent that reaches a point where it is construed as a threat to the "Church" is not tolerated. Heresy must be confined to the diffuse end of the intellectual spectrum or as Andrei Amalrik, author of *Will the Soviet Union Survive Until 1984?*, discovered, the KGB will come!

It is obvious that real tyranny of the mind persists and will persist so long as the hierarchy maintains its positions of absolute power and privilege over its citizens. This is the same sad pattern of centuries gone by.

State religions in democracies like Sweden and Britain are largely token. Here as in a few other cases there have been democratically elected and rejected governments bearing the socialist label. Here the objections to real socialism are pragmatic and instrumental, having to do, as I have shown, with the ineffectiveness of policies of public ownership. So long as socialism is confined to small doses and is more concerned with social justice than with public ownership, it is compatible with democratic values. But the extreme case of socialism, Soviet totalitarianism, takes us far beyond these pragmatic arguments. Totalitarianism of the left or of the right is essentially one phenomenon. It rests upon a basic contempt for individual significance and freedom. Fascism, Naziism, Leninism or Maoism are all essentially the same in that regard. They represent as much choice as that facing the heretic of the middle ages who would decide whether to be burnt by the Catholics or by the Protestants.

Notes

1. Saul K. Padover, *Thomas Jefferson and the Foundations of American Freedom*, (New York: Anvil Books, Van Nostrand-Reinhold, Co., 1965), p. 21.
2. Alfred North Whitehead, *Adventures of Ideas*, (New York: Mentor Books, 1964), pp. 75-93.
3. J. Huizinga, *The Waning of the Middle Ages*, (New York: Anchor Books, Doubleday & Company, Ltd., 1924), p. 18.
4. Quoted in Crane Brinton, *A History of Western Morals*, (New York: Harcourt Brace Jovanovich, Inc., 1959), p. 210.
5. Herbert J. Muller, *Freedom in the Western World*, (New York: Harper & Row, 1963), p. 90.
6. Roman Rakhmanny, *"Church-State Relations Live Issue in Kremlin,"* The *Ottawa Journal*, November 1, 1969.

PART THREE

An Improved
Liberal Approach:
Private Capital

Introduction

It is one thing to argue against any fundamental alternative to the private capital system. It is quite another thing to recognize soberly the shortcomings of that system and to devise improvements. I am no socialist, as the reader may have gathered by now, but I do share the conviction that we face serious problems and that our leadership has been sadly deficient in dealing with these. Where I depart from socialism is in refusing to substitute one set of outmoded doctrines for another.

The central economic problem remaining in the private capital economy is the inflation-unemployment syndrome. One basic policy objective of this book is to suggest a solution to this problem. As I hope to make clear, such a solution depends on the recognition that inflation and unemployment are not accidents or merely bad fortune but rather are outgrowths of basic structural changes in the private capital economy. Good theory must precede good performance.

Chapter **10**

The Mathematics
of Inflation

In a private capital system, under certain assumed conditions, the rate of change in the price level will reflect the difference between the average rate of change in money wages, including fringe benefits and the average rate of change in the production of goods and services. Stating this symbolically we have $P = W - Q$ where P is the rate of change in the price level, W is the average rate of change in money wages, and Q is the average rate of change in real output of goods and services per worker in the labour force.

The first of the "assumed conditions" referred to above is full employment. This varies in definition from country to country but is the condition which would be considered "normal" in any given country.[1] Usually the number of employment opportunities existing at any time would be in approximate equilibrium with the number of people available to fill them. Although I state full employment as a condition I am not convinced that the formula would be greatly affected by a condition of something less than full employment.

The second condition is the pursuit of a neutral monetary

policy. This would be the natural complement to full employment. It assumes that the monetary supply will be changed at a rate which will neither "overheat" nor "cool" the economy. This entails a modest monetary expansion sufficient to provide the aggregate demand consistent with rising output, without exceeding the limit where classic demand-pull inflation takes hold.

The third condition concerns the effect of factor costs due to imports. The assumption is that the price of imports will change at the same rate as domestic prices so that no country will import inflation. In some countries this is a significant factor while in others it has little influence. In most cases the influence of imports on consumer price indices is far less important than domestic cost factors.

Even though few countries have consistently pursued full employment and neutral monetary policies, the average results computed for fifteen O.E.C.D. countries for a nine-year period bear out the P = W − Q relationship quite well.

Table I[2]

	(1) P	(2) W	(3) Q	(4) W-Q	(5)	(6)
	(Prices)	(Wages)	(Produc-tivity)	Difference between 1 & 4		Unemploy-ment
Austria	2.9%	7.8%	4.5%	3.3%	−0.4%	2.4%
Belgium	2.1	6.6	3.3	3.3	−1.2	2.2
Canada	1.8	3.6	2.0	1.6	0.2	5.4
Denmark	4.1	9.1	4.0	5.1	−1.0	1.5
France (1959-)	3.8	7.0	4.8	2.2	+1.6	0.5
Germany	2.4	8.6	5.2	3.4	−1.0	1.2
Ireland	3.2	7.2	3.2	4.0	−0.8	2.8
Italy	3.4	7.3	6.5	0.8	+2.6	4.0
Japan	4.3	8.8	8.2	0.6	+3.7	1.0
Netherlands	3.2	8.1	3.4	4.7	−1.5	0.9
Norway	3.4	6.7	3.8	2.9	+0.5	1.0
Sweden (1961-)	4.1	8.2	3.3	4.9	−0.8	0.4
Switzerland (1961-)	3.4	5.6	3.4	2.2	+1.2	0.1
U.K.	2.8	4.3	2.5	1.8	+1.0	1.7
U.S.A.	1.5	3.2	2.7	0.5	+1.0	5.3
Aggregate Average	3.1	6.8	4.0	2.8	0.3	2.02

Showing:
a. Average Annual Increases of Consumer Prices, Industrial Wages and Productivity. (Columns 1, 2 and 3).
b. Relationship between formula P = W − Q and actual figures for countries surveyed. (Columns 4 and 5).
c. Average Unemployment as percentage of Total Labour Force (Column 6). *(Computed for 15 OECD countries 1958-1966)*

It should be noted that not all the fifteen countries achieved their norms of full employment. The average rate of unemployment, as shown in the table, varied from a low of 0.1 per cent for Switzerland to a high of 5.4 per cent for Canada. This is a significant variation.

Obviously under these circumstances not all Central Banks pursued neutral monetary policies. The performance has varied considerable partly due to the complexity of monetary influence. While it does make some difference whether a policy of "restraint" or "relaxation" is in effect, much depends on the timing and duration of the policy. There is a delay between cause and effect. Moreover, recent experience in Canada and the United States raises some doubt about the effectiveness of monetary policy in dealing with inflation. Even policies of severe restraint have had only modest success. Experts continue to look for signs of improvement but as time passes the signs become increasingly obscure. They approach the point of invisibility for the average housewife with 20/20 vision and 20/30 purchasing power.

A final comment must be made concerning the data employed in the table. Unless you are in a position to gather raw data – and that is far beyond the resources of an individual – you must make use of available data. In this case there are minor variations from country to country in the statistical definitions of unemployment, consumer goods and wages. Some O.E.C.D. countries report average wage "earnings" while others report average "rates." The wage data refers generally to the "industrial" sector of the economy but there are variations in the inclusiveness of that term. Finally, the wage package includes fringe benefits in some cases but not in others. These vagaries in the data require that we approach the results with caution and view them as approximations or tendencies. Having said that we may still note the proximity of formula and figures.

Economics is not a precise science. There are far too many variables to expect the real world to conform exactly to a model. Nevertheless, I have concluded that the relationship $P = W - Q$ is a useful guide in determining policy. Furthermore, if zero inflation is an objective to be pursued – as I argue it is — then the required relationship between W and Q is obvious. Because I believe that the latter is the dominant and dynamic element in contemporary inflation, I have included a series of graphs which illustrate the point.

Notes

1. The meaning of the word "normal" may be somewhat ambiguous. Canadian unemployment since the war has averaged between 4 and 5 per cent. In my opinion this level is far too high. We might realistically aim for a norm of 2 to 3 per cent.
2. (Table I) *Prices and Wages*
— O.E.C.D., *Main Economic Indicators 1957-1966*, Paris, April 1966.
— O.E.C.D., *Main Economic Indicators*, Paris, Feb. 1970.
— Annual % increases were computed directly from the published index numbers for "Consumer Prices Total" and Wages. The *Wage* indices referred in most cases to "Average Monthly Earnings". In the case of France, Italy, Netherlands, Switzerland and the U.K. they referred to "Average Monthly Rates". The definition of wage sector varies somewhat but generally refers to "Industry" including Manufacturing, Mining and Utilities excluding Construction.

Productivity
— O.E.C.D., *Statistics of National Accounts 1950-1961*, Paris, 1964.
— O.E.C.D., *National Accounts of O.E.C.D. Countries*, Paris, 1969.
— O.E.C.D., *Labour Force Statistics 1956-1967* Basic Statistics, Paris, 1969.
— O.E.C.D. Productivity data was directly available only for Canada and the United States. Productivity was computed for all cases by dividing *GNP at 1958 Prices* by *Total Labour Force*. These figures were then used to compute annual increases.

Unemployment
— O.E.C.D., *Labour Force Statistics 1956-1967* Basic Statistics, Paris, 1969.
— O.E.C.D. Unemployment *rate* data was available for only a few countries. Figures were computed by dividing "unemployed — registered thousands" into "total labour force." The results were close to published O.E.C.D. figures, but slightly lower. The reason for this is that the O.E.C.D. rates were expressed as a % of Civilian Labour Force while the computed rates were expressed as a % of Total Labour Force.

3. (Graphs) "Percent" refers to the percentage change in prices and wages from one year to the next. O.E.C.D., *Main Economic Indicators 1957-1966*, Paris, April, 1966 and *Main Economic Indicators*, Paris, February, 1970. With the exception of Switzerland all graphs cover the period through the first 3 quarters of 1969.

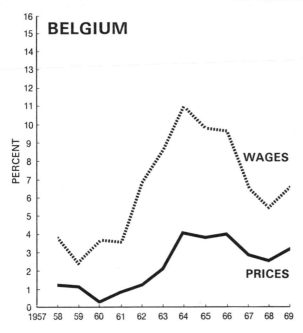

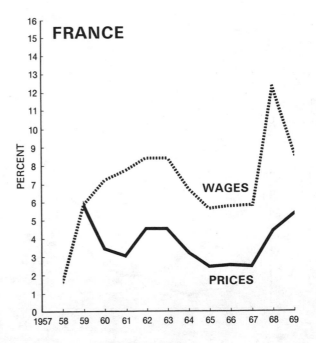

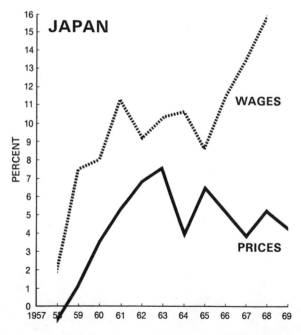

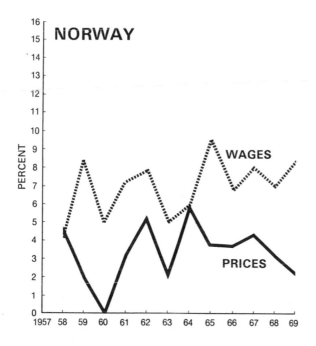

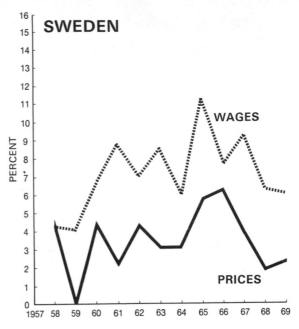

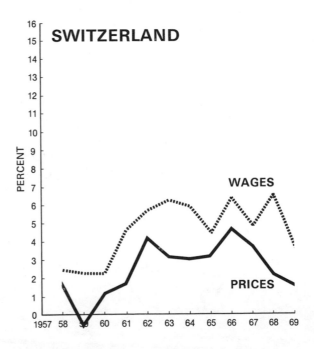

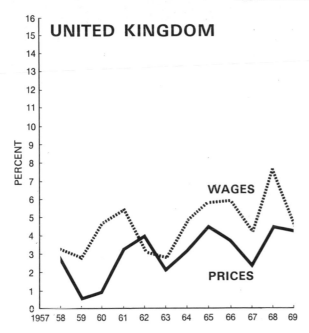

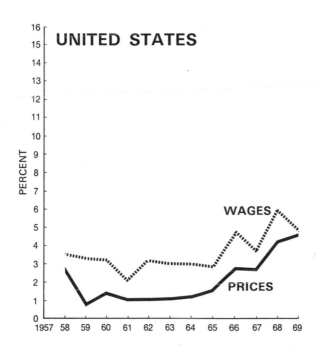

Chapter **11**

The Causes of Inflation

Since the Middle Ages, there have been problems and recurring crises associated with monetary inflation. Henry VIII was a master of the art of currency debasement. In 1542-43, for example, for each 100 shillings of the old coinage he made 120 shillings of the new. After keeping the extra 20 shillings for his personal use, he generously handed back the 100 debased shillings to his loyal subjects. No doubt an inflation resulted from this little exercise in "conversion."

There have been a number of cases of spectacular inflation. Such was the experience during the French Revolution and later in Germany and Russia after World War I. More contemporary examples can be found in a number of South American countries. Brazil, Chile, Bolivia, Uruguay and Argentina have each averaged more than 25 per cent annual inflation from 1950-1968.[1] In each of these cases, the inflation has conformed more or less to the classic definition of too much money chasing too few goods.

Less obvious but, nevertheless, persistent inflation has become the "norm" of modern society. Of course, there have been exceptions, particularly in the downturn of a business cycle during a recession or depression, but the longer term trend has been continuous depreciation of the unit, i.e., of a persistent rise of prices expressed in terms of the monetary unit.

The inflation rate in most western countries since World War II has varied considerably from zero or less to a high of 7 or 8 per cent annually. As long as the rate did not exceed 2 to 3 per cent, no one seemed too worried. This was particularly true in conditions of full employment. When everyone is working, the small redistribution of incomes that usually results from 2 to 3 per cent inflation is often a subject of discussion but seldom a question of urgent action. Those groups who receive a smaller share of the national income are usually unorganized or poorly organized and seldom generate enough political pressure to force a redress of the balance. Consequently, inflation rates of 2 to 3 per cent have become generally acceptable and are often referred to as normal by politicians and economists.

Since 1965-66, the inflation rate in Canada and the United States has started to climb. This has attracted attention and become a matter of current controversy. The redistribution of incomes has caused severe hardship for people working for low wages, for some groups of unprotected farmers and for old age pensioners and others living on fixed incomes. They have become much more vocal and, although they still lack the organization to exercise much political muscle, their plight has been recognized by idealists and humanists, who are themselves members of the more affluent sector, anxious to join and lead the battle.

The Bank of Canada and the Federal Reserve Board, recognizing the problems caused by inflation and concerned about the consequences, decided to exercise what they euphemistically refer to as "monetary restraint." This means slowing down or stopping the expansion of the money supply. The object of the exercise is to "cool" the economy and retard inflation.

Working slowly at first, because there is a time lag between cause and effect in these operations, and then more quickly as the full force of the "restraint" takes effect, the desired result is achieved. The economy is "cooled" to the point where it teeters on the precipice of a mild recession. Sale of luxury goods declines. Automobile sales reach the lowest level in years. Un-

employment rises to the highest rate in a decade. Hundreds of thousands join the ranks of the poor by being jobless.

To the extent that total demand is reduced and people put out of work, the policy of monetary restraint does have some influence on prices. In monopolistic and oligopolistic industries, however, the effect is negligible. As long as costs, including wages, continue to rise, prices continue to rise. Consequently, monetary restraint has not had anything like the success in controlling inflation that its promoters hoped for. Some monetary managers see slight signs of a slowing down of the rate of inflation. Others admit that the results have been disappointing so far but, due to the lag, the real results cannot be expected for a few months yet. The "restraint," meanwhile, must not be relaxed prematurely. The experts are barking up the wrong tree. They are fighting the wrong kind of inflation and their exercise in restraint is "doomed" from the outset.

The monetary policy being pursued in Canada and the United States, and to some extent in other countries, is designed to combat classic inflation. It is supposed to ensure that there will not be "too much money chasing too few goods." In Canada, however, there is not too much money chasing too few goods. There is adequate supply in almost all areas of economic activity and a surplus in some areas.

A year-end (1969) report compiled by the Canadian Department of Industry, Trade and Commerce indicated that in a few industries substantial capital investment would be required in 1970 to provide capacity to meet growing demand. There was no indication of existing excess demand, however, except some temporary shortages caused by prolonged strikes in the summer of 1969.

As early as mid-1969, the Economic Council of Canada had begun – but only *begun* – to suspect that conventional wisdom and policies were inadequate both to the analysis and cure of our inflationary woes. Its report of that year contrasted the inflation of "excess demand" in 1965 with the situation in 1968 and 1969:

Prices for various materials used in production – for example wood products – rose sharply, and interest rates and the costs of financing reached record levels. Total wages and salaries

increased by nearly 9 percent; average hourly earnings in manu-
facturing increased by 7½ percent; and increases in base rate
wages and salaries negotiated in collective agreements, although
marginally lower than in 1967, still averaged about 8 percent
per year over the life of the contracts.

In contrast with unemployment in the range of 4 to 5 per-
cent in 1968 and early 1969 [Oh happy days!], it is difficult to
argue that excessive general demand pressure has contributed to
inflationary conditions. The general policy environment in 1968
in Canada has been restrictive. There has been a significant
degree of fiscal restraint, as indicated by the $800 million sur-
plus in the government sector on a National Accounts basis in
1968. In addition there was some tightening in monetary and
credit conditions in the early part of 1968 in the wake of tempo-
rary strains in the balance of payments and, even more espe-
cially since the end of 1968.[2]

Having recognized the problem – and its novelty – the
Report then provides timid explanations. The cause, it argues,
may be "inflationary psychology." Big business and big labour
anticipate inflation, adjust their demands and thus set the stage
for the next round. Precisely! But what the Council does not
say is that this power to anticipate inflation, despite prevailing
unemployment and economic slack, is the characteristic of the
"new industrial state" which renders the traditional inflationary
tools ineffective. In a competitive market there is no "psychology." There is only supply and demand. But in the new industrial state there is "psychology" which, in fact, is only a
euphemism for *monopoly power*. It is not psychology that
anticipates. It is power.

The other explanation of our inflationary "lags" given by
the Council was growing inflationary pressures from the United
States. The debate about whether we have imported our inflation is still hot and furious. However it is resolved, the traditional
theory does not benefit. It is the thesis of this book that the
modern problem of inflation is not confined to Canada nor is the
orthodoxy of experts. It is a damn poor defence to argue that our
policies have failed because the same policies have been followed south of the border!

It is true that demand pressures remained a problem in the

United States longer than they did in Canada, and no doubt the financing of the Vietnam War played a role in that. By early 1971, however, those forces were ancient history. Defence spending had been substantially reduced over the previous two years. No outright shortages of any significant goods or services appear to have occurred in 1969 or 1970. Only two temporary shortages of nickel and copper were sufficiently serious to prompt the consideration of releasing quantities of these metals from United States stockpiles. In both cases, the metals were available but the demand was strong and the supply short largely due to strikes. Once the strikes were settled, the supply situation began to improve and recent reductions in the price of copper would indicate that the disequilibrium was quite temporary in nature.

The general economic situation in the United States was described by the *Survey of Current Business* in its year-end review. It observed that "overall economic activity in 1970 proved weaker than had been expected." Unemployment rose, capacity utilization sank, profits shrank. And yet, in the words of the review "the stubborn rise of prices, well after excess demand had been eliminated, was painful and frustrating."[3] Having said that, the review goes on to say, in words reminiscent of our own Economic Council, that "the economy had experienced years of serious inflation which worked its way deeply into the cost and price structure as well as into attitudes." In place of the word "attitudes" the reader may safely substitute the good old Canadian phrase "inflationary psychology". In place of both, please read *monopoly power*.

Even that bastion of orthodoxy, the United States Council of Economic Advisors, seems to have recognized some difficulty with the "demand-pull" thesis. Having dismissed wage and price controls, its 1971 report remarks that indeed "there are cases where price or wage increases not justified by competitive market forces are contributing to the prolongation of the inflation and to unemployment as well."[4]

It seems clear to me that we are dealing with something more than demand-pull inflation. That "something more" is not a temporary aberration but has to do with the basic structure of the modern industrial state. Our real problem in economic management is a traditional misunderstanding as to how our economy really works. The "lag" is not between policy and results but between reality and what goes on in our rulers' heads.

The classic treatment being prescribed by the orthodox bankers and economists assumes that the reduction in purchasing power will result in a reduction – presumably permanent – in rate of change in prices and wages. Some price reductions may occur in cases where a business or an industry is forced to liquidate an inventory. But these reductions will be minor, or temporary, or both. It is hard to imagine any measurable reduction in wages even in that part of the economy that is still subject to market competition. In the major industries, significant reduction in prices or wages is almost inconceivable. Can you imagine the United Automobile Workers agreeing to a reduction in pay merely because there happened to be 5 or 6 per cent of their fellow Americans unemployed? Can you imagine the Steel Workers of America being the first to volunteer? For that matter, can you imagine the banks reducing their service charges? None of these things is likely to happen with the present inadequate knowledge of economics.

The truth is that we have a schizophrenic economy. Or, if you object to the use of that word, you can just call it a dual economy. Part of it operates under classical market conditions, while much of the great industrial complex operates under conditions of oligopoly. A few giant corporations produce the major part of the total supply of a given product.

John Kenneth Galbraith describes this phenomenon in *The New Industrial State*.[5] I was a bit surprised that he used the greater part of a whole book to describe a situation that is obvious to the casual observer. He obviously believed that it was necessary to impress the fact on his fellow-professional economists and this inference depresses me considerably.

According to Galbraith, the giant semi-monopolistic industries do not price their products in a manner designed to maximize profits but are content with a return that will keep their shareholder owners quiet and at the same time permit growth of the company – a primary goal of the professional managers. The reason for this magnanimity is a bit obscure but certainly one could be forgiven for assuming that it was a policy of enlightened self-interest. Too high a profit margin would attract the curiosity of Congress or Parliament – with all the inevitable nuisance and embarrassment that could result. In addition, it would be an open invitation for excessive demands by labour and the possibility that acquiescence would affect the competitive position of company products both domestically and in export markets. But whatever the motivation – and it is not too important for our purposes – that is the way the system works.

When wage agreements are negotiated in these big industrial complexes, however, because the prices of products are below the level for maximization of profits, management is well aware that they can grant substantial increases and, under ordinary circumstances, pass the added cost along to the consumer. There exists a community of interest between management and labour that may not extend to society at large. In effect a collusion between employer and employee can be to the advantage – or at least to no detriment – of each but quite contrary to the public interest.

The pace-setting wage settlements granted in the semimonopolistic industries become the standard for all. "If steel can have it, why not me?" Pressure is exerted in the service industries for comparable increases and, if granted, substantial price increases occur. The reason is obvious. The big industrial complexes are the capital-intensive industries. They enjoy substantial increases in productivity largely, though not exclusively, attributed to the efficiency of the capital goods employed. Service industries do not have the same productivity potential. How many hair-cuts can a barber give in eight hours? How many pupils can a teacher cope with effectively? This year? Next year?

When large wage increases are granted in the service industries, the whole or a major part of the increase results in higher prices. The Japanese pointed this out to me from their experience. There the increase in productivity for heavy industry approximated, in percentage terms, the annual wage increases granted. But in the service industries, which demanded similar increases and where there was no comparable increase in productivity, the price rises were phenomenal. The average price increase of about 5 per cent resulted from trying to equate the two.

In Canadian and American experience, the story is similar. In 1966, the Canadian government granted the Seaway workers a 30 per cent increase over two years on the basis of a mediator's recommendation. The date appears to be a watershed on the economic graphs. Other Canadian unions demanded the same kind of treatment and many were successful. The new order of magnitude spread to the United States and, although it would be difficult to document, appeared to influence labour demands in that country. The result: a rapidly rising inflation, far more than either country had experienced since the Korean war.

It was at this point that the Bank of Canada and the Federal Reserve Board refused to finance full employment at the high inflation rate. Unfortunately, the strong monetary medicine they have been dishing out affects the wrong people. The huge industrial giants survive. They have financial power and if anyone is capable of additional financing, they are. Much of this strength comes from the large accumulations of retained earnings. It takes a long turndown to have much effect on them – except perhaps a temporary dip in profits. Similarly, their unions are pretty well immune. At least the men with seniority are. The new boys may be laid off for a while but after all they have few rights; with a few years' seniority, maybe, but not yet. And so the giants of industry slow down production and lay off workers when the economy is "cooled," but reductions in costs and prices are rare.

On the other hand, the free or market side of the economy gets it in the neck. It includes the farmers, the small businesses, the unorganized and the disorganized. It has more than its share of the under-educated and under-paid. When the going gets tough, it is the small businesses that have the most trouble with the banks. Banks are notoriously conservative and are not known for their humanitarian instincts. If loans are tight, it is the poor and marginal risks that receive the most "attention." Perhaps this is inevitable, but it results in a situation where the people least able to defend themselves are called upon to make the biggest contribution to an "adjustment" that was not of their making. The poor and the under-educated are the first to be laid off in a recession and they are the ones for whom the politicians and bureaucrats profess the greatest concern. God help us for we know not how to help ourselves!

It is difficult to know whether or not the central banking authorities realize what they are doing to us. Occasionally, the impression is given that they do understand and they are following restrictionist policies only with the greatest reluctance because the politicians are unwilling to face the gory prospects of admitting "cost-push" inflation. Ordinarily they give the impression that they really believe a substantial part of the problem is "demand-pull" and that monetary restraint is fundamental. This would seem to illustrate the lesson from economic history that the professionals are sometimes most reluctant to adjust their thinking to new conditions.

A recent confirmation of this professional conservatism was an interview – one of dozens I have had – with the Head of the Department of Economics at one of our universities. He felt that the policies being pursued by the government were correct. When asked how high the unemployment would have to go before the inflationary spiral stopped, he mentioned a figure of 10 per cent. I refrained from saying how naive I thought he was but I remember thinking that if that many people are thrown out of work unnecessarily by the high priests of orthodoxy, there will be a revolution – *even if I have to lead it.*

Not all central banks and governments are following the policies in effect in Canada and the United States. A number of interviews in the Nordic countries left me with the clear impression that they were more interested in relative than in absolute inflation levels. The Swedes, for example, said they were more concerned about the performance in Denmark, or Germany, or the United Kingdom, than they were in the absolute figures. If any one of these countries found that one of their competitors had achieved a markedly superior performance, they would be concerned. That is not to say that they were completely unconcerned about inflation, rather, they were more concerned about full employment and their position relative to their competitors.

The same is true on the other side of the world. There is full employment in Australia and New Zealand. In fairness, their inflation has not yet reached North American levels, although the trend is upward. Meanwhile, they are concentrating on growth, expansion and competition.

Japan is following a policy diametrically opposed to the policy in North America. The Japanese have a managed currency and they are not ashamed to admit it. So far, at least, the Bank of Japan has been willing to finance full employment with the rather high rate of inflation presently experienced. At the time of writing, there was not the slightest suggestion that they would consider changing their policy. Certainly, the Japanese policy makes more sense than the North American with approximately the same rate of inflation and a few million unemployed.

How long we will pursue our present policies, I do not know. At the moment of going to press, President Nixon announced a ninety-day freeze on all prices and wages. To be effective, this must be the prelude to permanent mandatory guidelines. This, in turn, requires better public understanding of economic fundamentals.

Assume that the year-to-year increase in production of all the people employed in producing goods and services averages 3 per cent. (This is the total increase in productivity attributable to the effectiveness of labour, the use of capital goods and improved technology.) Then if any person, or group of people, achieves a wage increase greater than 3 per cent, either a redistribution of income will occur (it will be at someone else's expense), or the increase will contribute to inflation (if full employment policies are pursued), or a combination of the two, which is what usually happens in practice.[6] This is not an abstract economic theory – it is a mathematical truism.

Notes

1. Econtel Research Limited, *World Inflation*, World Series #2, (London, 1969).
2. Economic Council of Canada, *Sixth Annual Review*, September 1969, pp. 147-48 and 149. The gap between actual and potential output—"economic slack"—has continued to grow to the point in 1970 where it represented a loss of approximately 3.5 billion dollars! Inflation did dip but appears to be on the rebound after the food price wars.
3. *Survey of Current Business*, January 1971, "The Economy in 1970," p. 17.
4. *Economic Report of the President*, "Annual Report of the Council of Economic Advisers," Feb. 1971, p. 80.
5. John Kenneth Galbraith, *The New Industrial State*, (Boston: Houghton-Mifflin Co., 1967).
6. This holds true no matter what distribution is in effect at the time.

Chapter **12**

Full Employment
Without Inflation

Taking into account the techniques that have been developed to maintain aggregate demand and to make sure that there is enough purchasing power to buy the total annual output of goods and services, and assuming the relationship between wages and prices, as suggested in Chapter 10, it is possible to consider a condition of consistent full employment with zero (or approximately zero) inflation. Theoretically, it can be done. All that is necessary is to maintain aggregate demand and to ensure that the average annual increase in money wages approximates the average annual increase in production of goods and services in real terms.

Whenever I make a statement like that, I remind myself of the story Mr. Justice Douglas C. Abbott of the Supreme Court of Canada used to relate, when he was Minister of Finance for Canada, about the man who drowned while wading across a river with an "average" depth of two inches. It is a good reminder because the case we are discussing is one where the variety of experience is very great and, consequently, the average a bit deceptive.

Generally, the greatest increases in productivity have taken place in the manufacturing industry. This is not surprising because it is in the manufacturing industry that very large investments of capital goods have been made. Another area of high productivity growth has been earth moving. Again, the marriage of man and machine has made it possible to perform the work of many. The change in agriculture can only be regarded as spectacular. In 1867, in Canada, "of a population of 3,690,000 more than 80 per cent were engaged in agriculture and extractive activities."[1] Today, less than 10 per cent produce a superabundance and soon 5 per cent will be able to provide us with all the food we require and more.

It has often been asserted that this increased productivity is due to more productive labour. One must be careful with semantics here. To the extent that labour is better educated and more skilful, it is more productive. And that is the trend. But the major causes of improved "labour" productivity are the use of capital goods and improved technology. The farmer who drives a powerful tractor pulling elaborate machinery produces much more than the same man behind horse and plow. It is the machine and, of course, the skill in operating it that makes the difference. A skilled labour force is essential, but beyond that wealth is a function of the great accumulations of capital goods and progressive technology.

It is in the service industries where productivity increases slowly, if at all. Barbers give about the same number of haircuts each year. I have seen the amazing performance described as a haircut given to United States Marine Corps recruits. It must be something of a world record for speed. Presumably all haircuts could be done that quickly. It is doubtful, however, that in a free competitive situation there would be much demand for this service. If long hair were not the vogue, and the fast clip was generally acceptable, it is difficult to imagine any improvement on Marine Corps productivity.

School teachers can only teach a limited number of pupils effectively. In some cases, classes are already considered too large. Clergymen can only make so many "visits" and deliver so many sermons each year; that is, if they want anyone to listen. Politicians can only answer so many letters, prepare so many speeches and cut so many ribbons each year. Modern transportation and efficient staff do speed them up but soon they reach the point of diminishing return. If you want another example, consider the house call of the doctor, plumber, carpenter or electrician. Traffic strangulation actually reduces the number of calls that can be made in a working day and consequently "productivity," in the sense of time available for useful work, actually declines. The results include soaring costs and in some cases the elimination of services. There are many other examples one could give to show that in some lines of work productivity is static or even on the decline.

At the same time, policemen, civil servants, preachers, teachers, politicians, doctors and others feel they should share in the general prosperity. They read in the newspapers or see reported on television wage and salary settlements in the manufacturing industries that may be as high as 8, 9 or 10 per cent per annum, or higher. Being human, they ask, "Why not me?" If steel or auto employees get 8 per cent, why shouldn't the postmen? After all, don't they carry that same heavy sack of mail every working day and get letters to their destination? Isn't their motto "neither snow, nor rain, nor heat, nor gloom of night stays these couriers from the swift completion of their appointed rounds."[2] It is a proud tradition and it deserves recognition — monetary recognition! Who wishes to be an economically second-class citizen? Certainly not the postmen and their fellow-sufferers and workers throughout the service industries.

Lacking any general formula or philosophy recognized by society at large, the strong unions took a perfectly natural position in demanding wage increases based on improved productivity in a plant or an industry. To the extent that they were successful, they unwittingly created a problem for society at large and, thus, indirectly, for themselves too. Other members of society began to ask for comparable increases when comparable productivity was not possible. Each group looked at the situation from its own point of view.

A moment's examination will show that distribution of increased productivity in the big industries to the employees of those industries alone would be a profound injustice. First of all, they are in a preferred position, because of their size and power, to set their own prices and know that they will be accepted by society at large. Second, the men who work in these industries benefit from the services of the other members of society such as garbagemen and postmen. In an interdependent society, they cannot get along without them. That is what the specialization of labour is all about. It would be quite unjust to require the men and women providing these services to work for wages and benefits grossly out of line with those received by the "privileged class" – the industrial workers. To be fair, there must be some sharing of benefits, some system of average benefits.

A quick examination will show that the costs of providing some services will never decline. Consequently, if the people providing these services share in the national productivity through wage increases, the price of the service provided will continue to rise indefinitely. At the risk of picking the wrong examples, but for the sake of illustration, this could be true for haircuts and some types of home repairs.

There are other services, and perhaps some goods too, where the rate of increase in productivity will be equal to the national average increase in productivity in real terms. In this category, wage increases can be granted at a rate equal to the national average without any price increases. The increased productivity takes care of increased wages and the return on capital invested.

Finally, there will be those industries where productivity gains will exceed the national average. This group can afford to pay wages that rise with the national average and reduce prices at the same time.

Two things should be obvious. First, the big oligopolistic industries can afford to reduce prices if their costs rise less than the increase in productivity. Adequate return on capital has already been provided so as to keep shareholders quiet and to finance continued growth. The increased profit that would otherwise accrue can be "shared" with society at large. Workers in the big industries would benefit, as consumers, and all other members of society would benefit proportionately. Second, unless some prices do come down incrementally on a continuing basis, there is no way, *repeat no way*, that the overall average price index can be maintained. If some prices must go up and others remain steady, it is axiomatic that some must come down to give an average of zero change, i.e. true price stability. Of course, there is a problem of the "weight" given to each component of a consumer price index, i.e. the proportion allocated to food, clothing, shelter, television sets, haircuts, etc.

A casual look at the composition of one or two indexes supports the contention that with average wage increases not exceeding the average increase in productivity, in real terms, true price stability is feasible. A dollar, franc, mark or kroner would buy as much this year as last year and as much next year as this year.

Notes

1. W.T. Easterbrook and Hugh G.J. Aitken, *Canadian Economic History*, (Toronto: MacMillan Company of Canada Ltd., 1961), p. 384.
2. From Herodotus, motto of U.S. Post Office.

Chapter 13

Why Not Creeping (2 Percent) Inflation?

Many orthodox economists have suggested that our system be stabilized at 2 per cent inflation. The Economic Council of Canada, in its *Sixth Annual Report*, suggested that this would be an acceptable figure. Why 2 per cent has been chosen, rather than 1 per cent or 3 per cent is hard to determine. Presumably because it is a nice round figure which is preferable to 4 per cent or 5 per cent inflation and which, at the same time, appears to be a reasonable target based on past experience.

In discussing this proposition with economists, I have found that there are two distinct schools of thought regarding the meaning of 2 per cent inflation. One school suggests that the total system be adjusted in such a way that there is a genuine equilibrium at 2 per cent inflation. That means that all the changes would take place necessary to eliminate any redistribution of income. The second school openly supports redistribution. The rationale for this is difficult to uncover but it seems intended as a concession to organized labour. Give labour a bit of advantage at the expense of the old pensioners and people living on fixed incomes, they say. The small advantage is presumably enough to get labour to play ball and the old age pensioners and widows have so little industrial and voting power that they can be expected to accept such a modest erosion of their purchasing power with only a "murmur" of dissent. This proposition is made as a pragmatic approach to the solution of real problems. Perhaps it is, but that does not make it right. And I, for one, would need a lot of convincing. The Economic Council of Canada did not indicate which of these two possibilities it had in mind.

Let us examine both cases. First, we will consider the situation where equilibrium is intended so that no redistribution of income takes place. Theoretically, there appears to be no reason why this cannot be done. It would require a consistent long-term policy decision, at the outset, meticulously observed by each succeeding administration. All pension plans would be rewritten in a way that would provide automatic adjustment equal to the 2 per cent inflation annually. This would apply to both public and private pension schemes without exception. All welfare and governmental transfer payments to individuals would be similarly adjusted.

Transactions between levels of government would be adjusted. All bonds and debentures would automatically be written at an interest rate 2 per cent higher than would otherwise be necessary. Bank interest rates would similarly be adjusted. The list of legislative and administrative amendments is a very long one, but presumably it is finite. Once the list had been exhausted, a process that could easily take several years to accomplish, the system would attain equilibrium.

At that time, wages and incomes would all rise by the average increase in productivity in real terms plus 2 per cent. Prices would rise, on average, by 2 per cent. Pensioners and others would be compensated for loss of purchasing power at the rate of 2 per cent. That would bring them back to square one. Everyone would be happy because no one would be worse off than the previous year and everyone would be handling more "paper" money.

The attractions of the system are obvious. But where is the advantage over an improved system with zero inflation? The advantages are all on paper. Without minimizing the attraction of the "paper" gains, I find it difficult to believe that the "dream world" would fool anyone very long. Once the economics of the system are understood – and this is fundamental to any equilibrium – I think most people will want to play it straight.

The second case of creeping inflation is one in which it is recognized, at least by the authorities, that a redistribution of income is taking place as a matter of national policy. Some groups in society are going to take more than a proportionate increase each year and, consequently, some are going to get less. For the sake of discussion, it does not matter which groups it will be. It could be the farmers, or Old Age pensioners, or people living on fixed incomes, or the unorganized, or someone else, but somebody is going to get the short end of the stick. The promoters of this suggestion must feel, consciously or otherwise, that inevitably it will be the weak who suffer but this really represents no change from the present situation and, consequently, this hypothesis is merely an accommodation to reality. One could introduce an air of nobility by observing that the weak and the poor would be better off with 2 per cent inflation than they are now with a higher rate. I guess the case can be described simply as "some improvement is better than no improvement." No doubt it is, but is it good enough? Since basic change is necessary in any case, why propose something that is fundamentally dishonest?

In a later chapter, we will look at some specific examples of redistribution and propose some improvements. I think some adjustments are essential. But to effect redistribution by means of inflation, especially when it aggravates an already bad situation, would be wicked. I can think of no other way to describe it. Destroying the purchasing power of one group in order to give special advantage to another group is dishonest. It is corrupt! It is every bit as bad as the practice of ancient kings who chipped a bit of gold from the coins of their loyal subjects in order to use it for their own purposes.

I would prefer to see any redistribution take place above board. Whatever it is, it should be understood, agreed and carried out in a straightforward manner. This can be done in a zero inflation situation. One group can be given more than another group, if that is policy, until an agreed distribution has been achieved. But everyone would know the object of the exercise and the results could be measured and understood. Surely that is better than dealing off the bottom of the deck.

I have examined the two variations of creeping inflation

carefully in my mind. Frankly, I can see no advantage in either case. Both contain an element of deceit. With zero inflation, any legitimate policy goals can be achieved. One group can be advantaged either temporarily or permanently if that is an agreed objective. Everyone, however, will know what is happening and presumably why it is happening. In addition, everything will be simpler. A 5 per cent coupon rate on a bond or debenture will mean 5 per cent. It will not be necessary to have 7 per cent mean 5 per cent in real terms. It will prevent also governments from taxing the 2 per cent inflation as if it were real. This has been, in effect, a tax on capital without the honesty of being described that way.

Psychologically, it seems to me that people could get used to an annual increase in real purchasing power of 3 per cent just as easily, or almost as easily, as they could to a 5 per cent increase of which only 3 per cent was real. So much depends on what one is used to – and the confidence in continuity.

It has been suggested that, should a national commitment develop to operate our economy at zero growth, it would be easier for governments if everyone got annual wage increases of 2 per cent, even though the 2 per cent would be pure inflation. My reaction to this suggestion is simple: if it is necessary to resort to money inflation to get national political support, then the policy does not really represent a national consensus. If, as a matter of choice, the majority wants zero growth rate, they should be willing to accept zero increase in wages. To expect more would not be rational. The necessity to reflect growth rates in wage increases would make it difficult for governments to maintain such a policy, except by genuine popular consent.

Believe it or not, I have tried to think of something good to say about creeping inflation. I have not succeeded. It is not necessary to the attainment of full employment. It distorts yardsticks of measurement in that standards are always changing rather than remaining constant. Inflation improves nothing, it adds nothing, it gives nothing. It is insidious and deceitful; consequently, it should be roundly rejected!

Chapter 14

The Regulation of Private Economic Power: The Anti-Combines Approach

I have attempted to show that, in the modern economy, economic power of huge corporations and unions contributes significantly to the problem of inflation and, thereby, unemployment. Further, I have argued that it is precisely those powerful organizations that are most resistant to the traditional monetary and fiscal policies. Since price stability is essential, it follows that new methods of public regulation are required.

According to "classical" economic theory, there should be no problem of regulation. The doctrine of perfect competition postulates a large number of firms and individuals engaged in the furious pursuit of self-interest. Out of their competition emerges a result that is automatically in the best interests of society at large.

As I have suggested earlier, the difficulty with this theory is that it does not correspond to the facts; at least, it does not correspond to all the facts. That there is some competition throughout the private capital economy is true. That there is close to perfect competition in some parts of the economy is certainly true. But that there is perfect competition in all important parts of the economy is manifestly false.

Faced with this situation, some argue: "If the problem is caused by huge corporations and unions, let us do away with them! Let us return post-haste to the days of pure and perfect competition." Before proceeding with my argument it is necessary to make clear why I think this approach is undesirable and, in fact, impossible. A brief history of anti-combines legislation in the United States and Canada will serve that purpose.

Monopoly Legislation in the United States

For a variety of reasons, the United States has generated more concern and literature about trusts and monopolies than any other country. There is no definite starting point for this concern but it did grow enormously until it became a major public issue in the latter half of the nineteenth century. That period saw the rise of new industrial combinations and trusts associated with such names as Rockefeller, Mellon and Carnegie and these in combination with business cycles and depressed agricultural markets generated a public outcry against the "new beast strangling the country." This was the rallying cry of populism.

The Sherman Anti-Trust Act of 1890 was an attempt to deal with this by legislation. It was a broad and, as it turned out, usefully vague document that declared illegal all trusts "in restraint of trade or commerce." Although its language was sweeping, its implementation apparently was more by way of placating the household gods than of actually ending the trusts. The debate that surrounded it in the Senate was, in fact, rather lukewarm and more than slightly hesitant. One American historian commented:

> *The Progressive discussion of the so-called Trust or monopoly question is . . . filled with all that uneasiness and inconsistency which we may expect to see when men find themselves enmeshed in institutions and practices that seem to be working to considerable effect but that violate their inherited precepts and their moral preferences.*[1]

That this was largely an ideological exercise is suggested by the fact that, in dealing with the trusts, the great "trust buster" Theodore Roosevelt tended to talk loudly and carry a small stick. And on more than one occasion, he ridiculed "the impossible task of restoring flintlock conditions of business sixty years ago by trusting only to a succession of lawsuits under the antitrust act."[2] For his part, Roosevelt had made the leap to distinguishing between good and bad trusts.

The courts, for their part, tended to interpret the new law in a way that was generous toward the practices and intentions of business. There were, of course, important rulings made against trusts but the basic approach was set down as the "rule of reason" in the Standard Oil Case of 1911. This important opinion stated that where behaviour was not specifically and intentionally anti-competitive, the test of reason was whether restraint quantitatively and substantially reduced competition.[3]

Curiously or perhaps not so curiously the Sherman Act came to be used with at least as much effect against unions as against trusts. The nineteenth century had been a period of difficult yet definite growth for unions and, quite naturally, they had pressed to be excluded from the provisions of the act. There were a number of amendments offered to that effect but for reasons that are not stated in the record the final bill made no mention of unions.

It was not long before the Sherman Act was added to the arsenal of weapons against unions. In 1908, the Supreme Court held that a strike and a secondary boycott by the United Hatters of America was in fact a "combination in restraint of trade" as prohibited by law. The gist of the argument was that union practices interfered with the right of both employer and employee to sell their commodities freely.[4] On this basis, court injunctions soon came into widespread use against unions.

The feeling on the part of labour leaders that unions were the victims of a double standard in the application of the Sherman Act led to their pressing a powerful campaign for amendment. This was paralleled by another wave of public sentiment against trusts and the result was the *Clayton Act* of 1914 which had two salient features. First, it added specific language to anti-trust law and it provided for an enforcement agency. Second, it declared "that the labour of a human being is not a commodity or article of commerce" and that unions should not be considered, per se, as conspiracies in restraint of trade.[5]

At the time, this act was hailed in some quarters as the magna carta of labour, freeing it from the paralysing effects of the injunction. In fact, there were loopholes in the law designed to protect property rights and in this way anti-trust continued to be used as a check on union development. In 1929, the American Federation of Labor published a list of 389 labour injunctions issued in the previous ten years by federal and state courts.

The power of unions continued to grow in fits and starts and, correspondingly, the law – legislation first, courts later – began to sympathize in fits and starts. The New Deal era did more to consolidate union strength than any other period before or since. In 1932, the *Norris La Guardia Act* established the general view that labour should have the right to organize "free from interference or coercion by employers . . . for the purpose of collective bargaining or other mutual aid or protection." It restricted the use of injunctions to clearly defined circumstances where "unlawful acts have been threatened or will be committed unless restrained" and where "substantial and irreparable injury to complainants property will follow."[6] In 1935, the *National Labor Relations Act (Wagner Act)* further specified and reinforced the same principles and provided machinery for their implementation. This was upheld by the Supreme Court with the dictum: "Employees have as clear a right to organize and select their representatives for lawful purposes as (a corporation has) to organize its business and select its own officers and agents."[7]

In effect, by 1940 the law had come to accept that the classical model of individual labourers selling their services individually had been superceded by new cooperative organizations. Furthermore, it was clear that the workings of these organizations would not be left to the market but would require some governmental regulation. In 1947, that regulation attempted to redress what was claimed to be an imbalance in favour of unions and to guarantee limited rights of individuals to opt out of unions.[8] But the principle of union organization was, and remains, the norm against which individual claims were judged. Regulation rarely speaks of monopoly any longer but rather distinguishes, as Theodore Roosevelt did for trusts, between good and bad unions and acceptable and unacceptable union activity.

The difficulty of enforcing anti-monopoly ideas against unions was not only a result of the growing power of labour. It was also that the ideology of pure competition was under attack from the facts of corporate growth. If the modern corporation was to be partially exempt from the workings of traditional economic theory, then why not the modern union as well? In 1957, John Kenneth Galbraith suggested the obvious rationale of big unions. They were simply, he argued, labour's appropriate countervailing power to big business and in that sense they were the heirs of the tradition of competition under new conditions.[9]

The attempt to regulate the bigness of business has met with enormous difficulties and increasing scepticism. In 1936, the *Robinson-Patman Act* stiffened the provisions relating to price discrimination by forbidding chain retail stores from setting lower prices made possible by mass buying. This was, of course, a laudable attempt to protect the corner grocery store but since this was to be achieved at the expense of the consumer it raised some difficult questions. If pure competition was indeed the guarantor of lowest prices, why was such regulation necessary?

The efficiency of the new economic order was and remains one of the perplexing difficulties that face the old ideology. The provisions of the *Celler Anti-Merger Act* of 1950 illustrate other difficulties. This amendment to the Sherman Act prohibits not only the acquisition of stock but also "the use of such stock by the voting or granting of proxies or otherwise" and the acquisition of "the whole or any part of the assets" of a competing corporation.[10]

Anyone familiar in the slightest degree with the recent business history of the United States may reasonably doubt the effectiveness of these provisions. There have been court actions and, among these, some sustained. But the problems of the law are enormous. First, there is the problem of defining "competing corporation," entailing as it does the more basic problem of defining markets and competition. The recent "vertical" merger movement has queried anew whether competition can meaningfully be confined to firms producing similar products. Second, there is the problem of enforcement since business has shown itself to be every bit as ingenious as the law. Consequently, prosecution has tended to occur only in the most blatant (careless?), but not necessarily most significant, cases. Finally, the law is enforced in the regular courts which, aside from enormous workloads, have limited training in the making of such basic economic judgments, as judges themselves concede.

The consensus is that these difficulties have been crucial and that therefore the anti-trust laws have, broadly speaking, been ineffective. In a 1949 symposium of public officials and economists, all the major participants were in agreement on that.[11] They differed only in answering why. Arthur Burns, a card-carrying member of the establishment, stated: "we have failed to achieve a competitive system" and he laid the blame for the ineffectiveness of the law on faulty economics. Contrary to accepted wisdom, he argued, efficiency may rest with size and in any case the courts are justifiably reluctant to substitute their judgment for that of businessmen.

The current thinking in the United States as regards big unions and big business would seem to be this. They are here and their coming has transformed society. Their benevolence to the public good cannot be taken for granted but neither is there available any longer a simple and coherent economic doctrine for judging them. In this, as in so many other areas, we are left to *ad hoc* intelligence which is well represented by Galbraith's dictum on market power.

The mere possession and exercise of market power is not a useful criterion for anti-trust action. The further and very practical question must be asked: Against whom and for what purposes is the power being exercised.[12]

Teddy Roosevelt knew as much sixty years before.

Anti-Combines Legislation in Canada

Generally speaking, the developments in the United States have come to pass in Canada, although at a somewhat later date. Thus Canada too has its large corporations and big unions and government has attempted to regulate these with similarly questionable success. One important factor which is peculiar, at least in degree, to the Canadian case is the large presence of foreign affiliates. This has meant the entanglement of "domestic" regulations with international considerations.

The history of Canadian anti-combines legislation begins in 1889 with the passage by Parliament of *An Act for the Prevention and Suppression of Combinations in Restraint of Trade*. The passage of the Sherman Act in the United States in 1890 seems to have stemmed from the same concern. During the debate on the Hill, one M.P. complained bitterly of "these men who have formed their illegal combinations and who come down with a great army of lawyers from Montreal and Toronto and with amendments carefully considered, to legislate this bill out of existence."[13]

The Act was substantially like the Sherman Act in its language and provisions. It listed a variety of basic practices that were prohibited but it provided no enforcement machinery. During its first ten years there was no successful prosecution under it and there was slight demand for more. The Liberal party felt that the basic remedy was not anti-trust law but rather, as in the case of Great Britain, the elimination or reduction of tariffs.

The next step came in 1910 with the passage of the *Combines Investigation Act*. Largely the work of Canada's first Minister of Labour, MacKenzie King, it provided procedures and machinery for the enforcement of the law. However, these procedures may strike the contemporary reader as slightly quaint. Under the Act, any "six British citizens" might make application to the courts for the investigation of combines. If good cause was shown a judge could then order an investigation and publish the results.[14] Subsequent history suggests that there were not many British citizens eager to do their duty.

The Canadian approach to these questions was suggested by Mr. King in presenting the bill. Like his colleague to the south, Mr. Roosevelt, he indulged in no sweeping condemnation of trusts but differentiated between the good ones and the bad ones. And the formula for enforcement was publicity and conciliation resting on the conviction that "light is the sovereign antiseptic and the best of all policemen."[15]

Notwithstanding this faith in light, subsequent legislation has opted for a bit more flesh, though only a bit more. In addition to attempting clarification of what a combine was, the revised *Combines Investigation Act* of 1923, which is the basis of present law, provided for permanent officers and staff and gave independent powers of initiative to that staff. Despite these powers, from 1923 to 1959 there were only sixty-five reports issued and twenty-three convictions. One non-admirer of the law has observed with perhaps more than a trace of bias:

> *Either Canadian business has been very good or our administration has been very loose. In either case, business seems to have little to worry about whether or not the law be strictly construed.*[16]

Amendments and additions to the law since World War II have been directed more toward clarification and guaranteeing fairness than towards stiffening its application. Following a parliamentary investigation of 1952, the agency was divided into two parts: one, The Director of Investigation and Research, to do basic and case research; the other, The Restrictive Trade Practices Commission, to hold hearings and to report to the Minister of Justice. Higher fines were added to the Act as well as specific prohibitions against resale price maintenance. The latter provisions, however, were considerably diluted by a subsequent revision of the law in 1960. In addition to giving some support to manufacturers by prohibiting sales below suggested manufacturers' prices, exports were exempted from the law as were six types of cooperative business practices, for example, the sharing of basic statistics. In short, there is not much evidence in Canada of a strong desire to enforce a truly strict anti-combines law and there is correspondingly little evidence that the law up till now has been noticeably effective.

The reasons for this are essentially those outlined in the case of the United States. On the one hand, it is exceedingly difficult to enforce these laws through the courts and this difficulty is compounded in Canada by the presence of international corporate structure. On the other hand, it is even more difficult to "argue with success" and there are few who deny that Canadian business, however organized, has been delivering the goods. American, British and Canadian history suggest that business has been genuinely vulnerable to such regulation only when times have been bad.

What of the applicability of anti-combines law to Canadian unions? As in the other cases, early legislation and common law applied strong "anti conspiracy" tests to union organization. And again, as in the other cases, these tests were gradually modified or overcome, although this process was not completed in Canada until after World War II. By then, Canadian labour too had achieved its magna carta of legislative sanctions. As for the Combines Investigation Act, it specifically provides that "Nothing in this Act shall be construed to apply to combinations of workmen or employees for their own reasonable protection as such workmen or employees."[17] Although the word "reasonable" is a catch, nothing has been caught on it and at least one author thinks that the labour exemption is too broad.[18] Of course, it must be added that this exemption does not mean that there is no law in Canada regulating trade unions.

There is good reason to conclude that traditional combines theory and law cannot provide an adequate basis for the future regulation of business or labour. The time has come to substitute a concept that is contemporary and that recognizes the economic facts of life. Big business and big unions are here to stay. Rather than delude ourselves that we can legislate these giants into the practice of "free competition," we must admit their existence and settle for appropriate regulations. These can be devised to permit a wide range of freedom to business and labour but still make monopolistic power in the hands of both subject to the test of the public interest.

Notes

1. Richard Hofstadter, *The Age of Reform*, (New York: Alfred A. Knopf, Inc., 1955), p. 245.
2. Quoted *Ibid.*, p. 246.
3. Summarized in E.V. Rostow, "The Development of Law on Monopoly and Competition," p. 169, in Alex Hunter, ed., *Monopoly and Competition: Selected Readings*, (London: Penguin Modern Economics Series, 1969).
4. Loewe V. Lawlor, 208 U.S. 274 (1908) summarized in Nicholas S. Falcone *Labor Law*, (New York: John Wiley and Sons Inc., 1962).
5. *Ibid.*, pp. 54-55.
6. Quoted, *Ibid.*, p. 572.

7. *N.L.R.B. vs. Jones and Loughllin Steel Co.,* 301 U.S. (1937) quoted Falcone, *Labor Law,* pp. 573-74.
8. *The Taft-Hartley Act.* American labor organizations have worked unceasingly for the repeal of this law, thus far without success.
9. "The Theory of Countervailing Power" in Alex Hunter, ed., *Monopoly and Competition,* (New York: Penquin Books, 1970), p. 123-39.
10. Summarized in Clair Wilcox, "Substantive Provisions of the Anti-Trust Laws" in Edwin Mansfield, *Monopoly Power and Economic Performance,* (New York: W.W. Norton and Co., 1964), pp. 117-125, p. 123.
11. "The Effectiveness of the Anti-Trust Laws." A symposium originally printed in the June 1949 issue of the *American Economic Review* and reprinted in a condensed form in Edwin Mansfield, *Monopoly Power and Economic Performance,* (New York: W.W. Norton & Co., Inc., 1964), p. 126-38.
12. "The Theory of Countervailing Power" in Hunter, *Monopoly and Competition,* p. 138.
13. Quoted in G. Rosenbluth and H.G. Thorburn "Canadian Anti-Combines Administration, 1952-1960." *Canadian Journal of Economics and Political Science,* Vol. 27, No. 4, (Nov. '61), pp. 498-508, p. 499.
14. As summarized in V.W. Bladen, "Monopoly and Competition in Canada" in Edward H. Chamberlin (ed), *Monopoly and Competition and their Regulation.* Papers and Proceedings of a Conference held by the International Economic Association, (London: Macmillan & Co. Ltd., 1954), pp. 3-20.
15. Quoted *Ibid.,* p. 19.
16. D.G. Kilgour "Combines-Fine Papers," *Canadian Bar Review,* Vol. 35, No. 9, (Nov. 1967), p. 1096.
17. From the Preamble, Sec. 4. The full text can be found as Appendix I in Richard Gosse, *The Law of Competition in Canada,* (Toronto: The Carswell Company Ltd., 1962), pp. 292-320.
18. See L.A. Skeoch, *Restrictive Trade Practices in Canada,* (Toronto: McClelland and Stewart Ltd., 1966), p. 4.

Chapter 15

Mandatory Wage and Price Guidelines

Huge corporations and unions cannot and probably should not be dissolved. At the same time, however, their influence on prices and incomes is often detrimental to the public interest. It is necessary, therefore, to implement wage and price guidelines.

Although I expect business and labour would cooperate in the development of an improved system, because they are law-abiding citizens for the most part, I am not so naive to think that they will do it voluntarily. All it takes is one greedy management group or one overly-ambitious union leadership to spoil the plan for everybody. One capitulation and all others feel the pressure to follow along in order to maintain their own authority and position of leadership. That is human nature. Consequently, the only workable solution involves making the price and wages guidelines mandatory.

More and more the necessity for price and wage guidelines is being recognized. One country after another is tip-toeing in that direction. So far, however, the voluntary method has been the predominant one in the private capital countries.

The effectiveness of the voluntary method is highly

questionable. After a year and a half of fitful attempts at voluntary wage-price guidelines, the Canadian Prices and Incomes Commission meekly withdrew to the library – to do research. The immediate cause was the refusal of business to cooperate with a six-month extension of voluntary price restraints. But this refusal was, in turn, conditioned by long-standing intransigence on the part of labour.

The interesting thing about the death of guidelines is that inflation was left alive and kicking. And the inference from that was drawn by Dr. Young, the Chairman of the Commission:

Without an early and substantial moderation of the size of wage and salary increases, and pricing policies which adequately reflect any moderation of cost increases . . . the choices will be renewed inflation, an unacceptable level of unemployment or compulsory measures of some kind.[1]

In the United States, a productivity-based wage-price guideline policy was introduced in the 1962 *Economic Report of the President*. Its objectives were full employment (set at 96 per cent), stable prices and an improved balance of payments. Its rationale was provided by the Council of Economic Advisers which saw inflation mainly as the product of the market power of big business and big labour.

Despite several years of exhortation with "civic responsibility" the favourite phrase, the policy soon came upon hard times. In 1966 it was "shattered" by a series of important collective bargaining agreements. Many prominent labour and business leaders pointed to this as the finale of voluntary guideposts.[2] So it was. But once again we note that the end came at a time when serious inflationary trends were becoming manifest.

It is obvious from this experience that voluntary restraint is extremely difficult to implement or maintain. By contrast, we may cite the case of Australia which has a long tradition of state intervention in wage settlements. This system comes very close to an acceptable definition of mandatory guidelines. Its results have been quite good.

Prices

At this point, I must make very clear what I mean by price and wage controls. First of all, regarding prices, I do not mean a system under which governmental bureaucrats set individual prices. I have had far too much experience in government and business to suggest anything so drastic and unworkable. That kind of intervention worked reasonably well during war, for a short time. Even then, distortions were created which would not have survived had World War II continued much longer. The short-term success of the programme, in Canada at least, was due largely to the fact that the "frozen" prices were in most cases those previously set by industry itself. These provided satisfactory margins if costs did not change materially and, when they did, it was normal to make allowances for the new cost structure. In the longer run, however, and especially in respect of new products, governments are not competent to set individual prices. I make this statement categorically.

A case in which I have personal knowledge may help illustrate the point. For a number of years after World War II, there was a desperate housing shortage in Canada – even worse than the one existing today. The Federal Government through its housing agency, Central Mortgage and Housing Corporation, decided to encourage new house construction. It did this by undertaking to insure high ratio mortgage loans made by insurance companies and others to builders and home purchasers. A condition of the granting of the maximum loan, however, was the right of the Central Mortgage and Housing Corporation to set the retail price of the house.

By the early 1950's, the market had eased to the point where the maximum price set by the Corporation became a minimum charged by the builders even though in many cases it was higher than would have obtained otherwise. At this point, I, among others, suggested that the fixed prices were no longer necessary. The Minister to whom Central Mortgage and Housing Corporation reported, the late Honourable Robert H. Winters, took the question up with the Corporation but the advice they gave him was highly negative – individual price-setting was to continue.

This was not the first time that, in my opinion, the Corporation had given the Minister poor advice. I asked the Minister if he would be interested in looking at the detailed cost records of the company that I was associated with at the time. He was interested, so I produced the cards that showed profit margins varying from minus $400 to plus $1,900 a unit, all on the basis of prices set by Central Mortgage and Housing Corporation. This ridiculous distortion created problems in site-planning, sales effort, etc. Company policy, to the extent it could be applied, called for a modest 6 to 7 per cent gross profit before taxes which meant roughly $650-$980 profit per unit. Minus $400 was too low; plus $1,900 too high. The Minister was impressed. About two weeks later, the fixed-end selling price was removed. New house prices in Toronto declined, on average, $300-$400 a unit in less than a month.

This story is intended to underline two points. First, govment is incompetent to set individual prices. Second, the pricing policy in the industry was calculated as cost plus a percentage markup to take care of the "profit" for rent on capital invested. The percentage markup shown above was probably too low to provide the kind of long-range expansion needed. Nevertheless, it probably would have been adequate on a fast turnover if mortgage money and serviced land had been constantly available. As it turned out, largely thanks to governmental incompetence, they were not always available.

The percentage markup on cost varies greatly from one business to another. Immediately after the war, my wife and I bought a ladies' ready-to-wear shop because a second-storey apartment was included and we were desperate for a place to live. The markup in that business was very high – from 33 per cent to 70 per cent on cost. But it was necessary because with style goods, the markdown on unsold merchandise is phenomenal. Dresses that had been in the store sixty days were often sold for cost – which meant, in fact, a substantial loss. In 1947, the introduction of the "new look" meant that our entire inventory was obsolete within a period of about thirty days. For months, any short girl who entered the store was literally besieged with attention as we tried desperately to dispose of the short dresses one by one. Now that I am safely out of the business, it is interesting to watch the mini, midi, maxi battle which has provided the trade with its worst nightmares in years.

These two examples – actually, rather extreme cases – give some indication of the variety of experience related to different kinds of business. Some have low markup,[3] and some high. Some can attract capital with a relatively low-profit margin. Others require substantial return on capital to persuade investors to participate; this is especially true where the risk involved is considerable.

Experience has shown the "order of magnitude" of the return on capital which is required for a particular industry to compete in capital markets. No single formula would apply in all cases and certainly I would not attempt to devise one. That is the kind of exercise that civil servants are competent to undertake (hopefully, in consultation and cooperation with the industry involved). There is no reason why, in cases where guidelines are applied, formulae cannot be devised that will accommodate the various requirements of different industries and still leave them the autonomy required for successful operation.

Wages

As with prices, government should not become involved in setting individual wages. It may be necessary to have some national guidelines for distribution, perhaps between trades and for different levels of skill within a trade. This is a function best performed by labour itself, however, perhaps through machinery set up by government.[4] Within a plant, individual adjustments should be made through direct management-labour channels. The only overriding criteria must be that the average annual increase must not exceed the average increase in physical output in real terms, i.e. the guidelines. And management should follow the same rules when evaluating its own contribution. One final caution applies to wage drift.[5] It must be confined to a "norm" and not used as a device to circumvent the guidelines.

It must be understood that the average annual increases referred to in the previous paragraph include fringe benefits. Fringe benefits often have a substantial monetary value, in some cases as great or greater than the increase in money wage itself. Too often, the powerful trade unions in the oligopolistic industries have been able to negotiate substantial benefits that are not available to many other workers. These include holidays with pay, severance pay, medical insurance, pensions, etc. In a truly just society, it would seem natural that many of these benefits should be guaranteed by statute and, consequently, available to all workers. In addition, to the extent that insurance coverage is required to provide an element of financial security in an impersonalized society, access to the insurance should be equal and universal. This basic security is so important that I will return to it in a later chapter. For the moment, however, I just want to emphasize the basic unfairness of a system where some workers get all the benefits simply because they work in industries that can pass the increased costs on to society at large while other workers have few, if any, of these same benefits even though they spend their lives providing services to the other "privileged" group.

Where Price and Wage Guidelines Apply

It is necessary to "control" prices or, if you prefer, apply mandatory guidelines, only in that part of the economy that I describe as rigid or semi-rigid. More precisely, guidelines must be applied to monopolies, oligopolies, cartels; in effect, in any case of "less than perfect" market conditions. This point of view has been expressed by others, including J. K. Galbraith who has promoted the idea vigorously in recent months.[6]

The list of industries varies somewhat from country to country. Illustrative is the group Galbraith cites in the United States: automobiles, aluminum, rubber, synthetic fabric, transportation, tin cans, chewing gum, glass, soap, breakfast food, cigarettes, most electrical goods, aircraft, tractors, computers, typewriters and most chemicals. The list for Canada would not be significantly different.

There will always be borderline cases. It should be possible for a company or an industry to opt for the free or the controlled system. In the case where the option is in favour of the controlled sector, it should have the protection of the law in respect to its "arrangements" with other companies because, presumably, the public interest will be satisfied by observance of the guidelines. Where the option is in favour of the "free" sector, however, the option should be easily subject to appeal when there is evidence of price fixing, identical bidding or lack of genuine competition. The public interest must be given the benefit of the doubt.

All wage increases should be subject to guidelines wherever a contract exists. There is no simpler test, nor one which is easier to administer. A "collective" agreement is subject to the guidelines.

Notes

1. *The Ottawa Citizen,* Dec. 2, 1970.
2. George Meany, Roger Blough and Neil Jacoby, *Government Wage-Price Guideposts in the American Economy.* The Charles C. Muskowitz Lectures, (New York: New York University, 1967). See the Forward by Abrahm Gitlow. The lectures by Meany and Blough are classic examples of labour and business passing the inflationary buck.
3. The leaders in the automobile and steel industries advise me that they too base their prices on cost plus a percentage markup — in the main.
4. This will be explored more fully in a later chapter.
5. Wage drift is a system of job reclassification often used to nullify the intent of wage restraint guidelines.
6. John Kenneth Galbraith, *The New Industrial State,* (Boston: Houghton Mifflin Co., 1971).

Chapter 16

Is It Possible?

Almost everyone I interviewed in the course of my research dismissed, out of hand, the possibility of operating a private capital system with full employment and without inflation. They assumed that the two were incompatible. On the few occasions when I pressed the issue the interviewee fell back on historical precedent as final proof. What *has* been *must* be. There was some embarrassment when this became obvious. A handful of other people who appeared to share my understanding of the modern economy concluded that however desirable it is in theory, it is impossible because big labour or big business will oppose it! Only one man with whom I spoke said that it would be just as easy to stabilize at zero inflation as at two per cent (the figure embraced by the orthodox). When I asked this man how many of his fellow economists agreed with him, he shrugged his shoulders and said "I suppose I'm a maverick."

The arguments against wage and price guidelines are of three kinds. First, there is the cry of the business and labour elites that such guidelines are a violation of the free enterprise system. Second, there is the argument, usually made by economists, that guidelines would prevent the mobility of labour and capital. Finally, there is the argument, almost always made by politicians, that the average citizen will not support such a programme. I would like to discuss each of these arguments in turn.

"Free" Enterprise

With many of my friends, opposition to price and wage controls borders on hysteria. It would, they say, be striking a mortal blow at the "free enterprise" system. Poppycock! There is nothing "free" about monopolies, oligopolies and cartels. Moreover, as far as the system is concerned, price and wage controls just might save the "private capital" system, which is presently going down the sink at a fair clip.

Only part of our system operates under market conditions. The most significant sector of the modern industrial state consists of the huge and powerful oligopolies – they are the "private capital" dogs that wag the "free enterprise" tail. For the dog, wage and price controls are the medicine that may save the whole critter.

The opposition to wage controls by some trade union leaders is just as wild. An unwarranted intrusion in the process of "free collective bargaining," they say. Nonsense! Free collective bargaining, in the modern context, is just as much a misnomer as Progressive-Conservative which really means standing with one foot on each of two horses going in opposite directions. Collective bargaining in the big industries is no more "free" than the price of steel or the price of cars. Big unions in big industries are monopolies. They are, in fact, the only source of labour. Can you imagine the automobile industry, or one of the big three, breaking a strike by recruiting an entirely new labour force including all the wide range of skills required. Not very likely!

Both the huge oligopolies and their equally powerful monopolistic labour unions follow practices that anti-combines legislation was intended to prohibit. The fact that decades-old exceptions given to the unions still apply and that the law never did adequately take the oligopolies into account is further witness to the theory that men move with incredible slowness in adapting their laws and institutions to changed circumstances. Our world changes and generations later, with approaching crisis, we begin to react.

Canadian legislation is based on the myth that we operate a market economy except for the illegal combinations and agreements in respect of price fixing. As a consequence, it is almost completely ineffective. Occasionally a prosecution is successful but the penalties provided by the law are minimal and fines fit into the penny-ante group.

The law is completely powerless insofar as the oligopolies are concerned. As long as they are careful – and they are – they do not come within its scope. Many of our prices are set by un-official agreement. No notes or records are kept which might be embarrassing or illegal. A wink is as good as a nod to a blind horse but a wink or a nod at an "association" meeting is well understood and without the benefit of fine print. Nearly every group has its own association – the bankers, the brickmakers, the paper-makers, and on and on it goes. It is a long list. In almost every case, agreed charges or prices are set in circum-stances of less than pure competition. The public interest has to be met but there is no law requiring it – for the banks or the unions.

There are precedents that could apply. The Bell Telephone System in Canada, for example, has both its individual rates and the rate of return on capital subject to review and approval by the Canadian Transport Commission. I am not suggesting that we go that far with the oligopolies. It would be sufficient to limit the rate of return on capital as a guarantee of the public interest.

Most important of all is the recognition that no new principle is involved in applying mandatory guidelines. It is merely the extension of existing and long-established principles into the contemporary situation. We have always said that we would not condone power groups manipulating prices in a way that was contrary to the public interest. And yet that is exactly what we have been doing for years – condoning it. We have to update our laws and our administrative machinery in a way that will give current meaning to our principles – and admit the facts as they exist.

Mobility of Labour and Capital

A number of my economist friends have expressed concern lest the imposition of mandatory price and wage guidelines introduce an element of rigidity into the system that would unduly restrict the mobility of labour and capital from one industry to another. Although I personally believe this concern to be exaggerated, I know it is a genuine concern and, consequently, one which cannot be dismissed out of hand.

In an absolutely free market economy, if such a thing were possible, labour and capital would move from the least profitable to the most profitable industries. Whether profitability and social desirability are coincident, however, is not always certain. It is possible that peddling flesh and pot might be among the most profitable industries – although it is difficult to say just what the relationship may be between high prices and scarcity of supply. These businesses are considered immoral in some circles and illegal in most jurisdictions and, consequently, the high return may be governed to a considerable extent by the risk involved and the monopolistic arrangements normally associated with these kinds of enterprises. To divert scarce resources from, say, pollution control measures to these other pursuits simply on the basis of profitability would be considered a backward step by some.

Nevertheless, assuming an enterprise is considered legal, profitability has been and will remain a most important consideration in the flow of labour and capital. Society has other means for judging social desirability and for exercising control if it is warranted. This can be accomplished through tax rates, credit regulations and other devices. But in most cases, these will have an effect on profitability and, consequently, they will exercise an indirect control on the allocation of resources rather than a direct control.

Within the system, therefore, profitability will continue to regulate the allocation of resources to a considerable extent. A new industry which its promoters expect to be profitable – hence their involvement in the first place – should be in a position to pay good wages. If it does, it will be in a position to compete for new entrants to the labour force. Also, to the extent that its wages are higher than those paid by marginal service industries, qualified workers will be encouraged to change employment in order to improve their position economically.

The same general remarks apply to capital. So long as a new industry is operating in the market – and that would be likely if its product was not protected by patent – it would be free of the guidelines. Consequently, its chances of exceptional, early profitability would be enhanced. Subsequent market competition would moderate those profits. If, as the industry matured, it came within the test of oligopoly it would also come within the ambit of appropriate guidelines. But as an established industry it should have no difficulty competing for either capital or labour. Its profitability will have been established. Its ability to pay higher wages than those of some service industries in the market sector, may be assumed.

The assumption may be spelled out. There will continue to be a margin between wages paid by the large industrial empires and those paid by small service industries. The size of the margin may be reduced. Indeed, some reduction is probably essential to the elimination of poverty and the realization of economic justice. But the possibility of eliminating the margin is highly remote and not necessary either for justice or workability. The system must remain dynamic. It cannot be entirely rigid. There must remain a sufficient spread between minimum wages and those available elsewhere to encourage and reward initiative.

Finally, we may cite an extreme case. If a new product or service was judged essential to the public interest at a time of scarce capital and human reserves, government could make an exception of it. The tremendous fiscal powers of government could be used to reduce the profitability of other less essential industries. In this way could not a pool of capital and labour be made available for a new industry without the traditional inflationary pressures? The temporary advantage would be sufficient to achieve the desired result. This would pose no exceptional problem – beyond the ordinary difficulties of the decision-making process.

It is difficult to foresee a situation requiring such special treatment. But if one did occur, extraordinary short-term measures could be adopted. These need not violate the guideline averages. The kind of fiscal measures required are quite well understood. What remains is only the will and the skill to exercise them.

In conclusion, I wish to repeat my conviction that mandatory guidelines need not unduly restrict the mobility of labour and capital, provided the guidelines are based on well-established experience in each area. As for the new or unusual circumstance, there is always common sense. This may be a bit optimistic, but I hope (and think) not unrealistically so.

The Ordinary Citizen

Finally we come to the argument that the ordinary workingman would never support wage guidelines. I think such an argument is tantamount to saying that the Canadian labourer is either stupid or immoral. I disagree emphatically. Without minimizing for one moment the formidable obstacles to progress in this area, I must say that in the final analysis I have confidence in both the good will and the good sense of working people. This is not just wishful thinking on my part. It is not based on an idealistic view of human nature. It represents a balanced judgment based on more than twenty years' experience as the elected representative of workingmen. I have a greater basic confidence in the intellectual integrity and common sense of workingmen than I have in academics, businessmen and politicians.

I have also developed a high respect for the stabilizing influence of the wife of the workingman. She knows first-hand the consequences of inflation. She knows first-hand the feeling of insecurity when the family income is cut off due to strike or lockout. I remember well chatting with a group of ladies in a Northern Ontario mining centre during an election campaign a few years ago. They understood the fundamentals. Higher wages were followed by higher prices. It was like a squirrel cage, they said. You get on and start running. The faster you run, the faster the cage turns. It is difficult to do more than stand still "relatively." These ladies knew that the system had to be changed and that it had to start somewhere. But no one wants to make the first move for fear that others will not follow and therefore one's relative position would suffer. In other words, the "pecking order" must be maintained and along with it the status quo.

After all, to expect a group that has been getting annual wage increases of 8 per cent to agree to accept 3 per cent is naive. It runs against the grain. The instinctive reaction is negative. The human animal is basically very conservative and does not like change. There is a fear of the unknown, a basic distrust. Even when the necessity for change is acknowledged, there is a profound inertia because most people "prefer the devil they know to the one they don't know." Change often occurs only years or decades after it is first required.

Change, however, must come! In countries like the United States and Canada where central banks have refused to finance full employment at current prices, the effects of the status quo are almost catastrophic. Hundreds of thousands are unemployed. The weak and the disorganized are trampled slowly underfoot. In other countries where central banking policy is designed to maintain full employment, but where there is a high inflation rate, redistribution of income is taking place in a way that is building time bombs of discontent for the future. The fuses are still unlit but, inside, the power of a potential explosion increases as some groups are consistently disadvantaged by their more powerful and privileged brothers.

When the mathematics are examined closely, large numbers of unionists will find that they would be as well off, in real terms, with smaller wage increases and no change in the price index. After all, what is the difference between an 8 per cent increase in money wages with 5 per cent inflation and 3 per cent increase in money wages with 0 per cent inflation? No difference! The relative advantage in real terms is exactly the same. Consequently, for millions of workers, there would be no disadvantage in switching to an improved system. They would not handle as much "paper" money but their purchasing power in terms of shelter, food, clothing and recreation would be just as great.

Of course, there are some groups who would be slightly less well-off if they accepted gains equal to the national average. They have been getting 1, 2 or 3 per cent above others in real terms. They are the strongest and most privileged, whether on the management or labour side. It would not be fair to be too critical of this group. They play the game within the rules of a "system" that permits them to use their power to their own advantage. In some cases, they may be quite oblivious of the consequences of their action for other people.

In countries with significant or high unemployment, the big winners from an improved system would be the unemployed. They would have jobs and opportunity. For the great majority who want to work, a job at a decent wage is one of the most fundamental and important "rights" in a civilized society. It is not just purchasing power that is at stake. There is a question of human dignity. There is a basic human need to make a contribution to society and, in return, to receive enough reward to keep oneself and one's family in reasonable comfort. Of all the problems in which I have been involved during my public career, none has bothered me more than the plight of able-bodied men who are not only willing but anxious to work but cannot find employment. I have seen men go to the employment office day after day tracking down every possible lead without success. I have seen the will begin to break after weeks or months of "failure" and I have seen the devastating psychological and family problems that develop in cases where hope has been abandoned.

Of course there are a few people who do not want to work, but these are rare cases. Nearly everyone is happier with something to do. Most unemployment is involuntary. There are some ingenious souls who can "manufacture" a job for themselves. (I have met quite a number in government.) But in periods of high unemployment there are many who simply cannot find work no matter how hard they try or how ingenious they are. To those who callously and ignorantly say that the unemployed are lazy I reply that if that is so Canadians are the laziest people in the industrialized world because we have the highest unemployment rate! In fact, it is not a case of laziness at all. It is a case of economic mismanagement. Periodic unemployment has been the curse of the private capital system. In retrospect and in the light of our present knowledge, this condition is positively and absolutely unnecessary!

Next to the unemployed, the big winners would be the retired, especially those people living on fixed income. In the past few months I have received an increasing volume of correspondence from Old Age pensioners who are suffering "the squeeze." Those who have no private savings and who rely completely on the non-contributory Old Age Pension are in a bad situation. In Canada, this pension has been increased by a maximum of 2 per cent annually in accordance with a cost of living clause inserted in the law in 1964. But this increase has been only a fraction of the loss through inflation. The fortunate few living in public housing fare better but the majority who have to find their own accommodation are in real trouble.[1] Other people with small industrial pensions or small savings have found these constantly eroded. The "adequate" provision they thought they had made for their old age turns out to be quite inadequate. These are victims of income distribution. They have been cheated by a society that does not understand the results of the inflationary "creep." An improved system would give Old Age pensioners the security and peace of mind that come with the knowledge that their purchasing power would remain intact.

In the constituency that I represent in the House of Commons, there are two large old people's homes. They are constant reminders of what it is to be old and poor. Some people find the problems of the old and their pensions a bit remote. But then the thought occurs that everyone is moving toward old age and a time when these difficulties will be real and pressing. By adopting an improved system now, we can help make provision for our old age. If we stop inflation, we will be able to predict with greater certainty the standard we will be able to maintain in retirement. Here is a possible benefit for everyone. Even the very strong who may have to accept slightly lower gains now will benefit when they retire. With improvements in medical science and longer years of retirement, this becomes a major consideration. People who have retired after contributing to the development of our society have a right to expect that we will take all reasonable steps within our power to maintain the value of their savings. To do less is to betray their past and our future.

It is in the self-interest of the overwhelming majority of our society to operate that society under conditions of full employment and stable prices. This is true both for those working and for those retired. The handful of exceptional cases would receive a benefit after retirement which would more than compensate for compliance. The average workingman is no fool. He is as aware of his self-interest as anyone; furthermore, he is as understanding and considerate of other groups in society as anyone. An improved system makes common sense. Consequently, I am confident that it will be easier to get the cooperation of the ordinary workingman than the cooperation of leaders of labour, business and government.

Notes

1. For example, the cost of *National Housing Act* bungalows rose by almost 25 per cent between 1965 and 1969.

PART FOUR

The Liberal Agenda

Introduction

It is my thesis that unemployment and inflation are the basic problems facing private capital economies. I have suggested what I believe must be done in order to solve these problems. I have stated the obvious rationale for action, namely that inflation and unemployment cause enormous hardship and uncertainty which, in turn, threaten the very stability of our political systems.

Looked at from another perspective, however, all of this is only a means to an end. It is the foundation upon which we may begin to construct adequate solutions to that series of challenges which will determine our social future. These challenges include poverty, preservation of the environment, urban development and security of the individual. It is my conviction that we cannot adequately confront these unless we have first established basic economic order. I have argued that this means mandatory wage and price guidelines.

Having stated the case for such a program I would now like to turn my attention to the challenges of the "liberal agenda".

Chapter 17

The Problem of Poverty

Poverty in Canada is real. Its number are not in the thousands, but in the millions. There is more of it than our society can tolerate, more than our economy can afford, and far more than existing measures and efforts can cope with. Its persistence, at a time when the bulk of Canadians enjoy one of the highest standards of living in the world, is a disgrace.[1]

The poverty situation in the United States is not very different from the Canadian situation described in the above extract. Even in the richest country in the world, there are millions of poor people, poor by any reasonable standard of judgment. And it is not only many blacks who are poor. There are millions of whites who are equally disadvantaged for one reason or another. Poverty knows no boundary of race, creed or colour.

My knowledge of poverty does not come from reading books but from first-hand experience with the problems of my constituents.[2] It has taken me right into the heart of problemland. Many of my electors pay 40 per cent or more of their income for shelter. One family in my constituency was seriously considering taking a teenage son out of high school because they could not afford shoes, clothes and a winter jacket for a fast-growing boy. This is only one example and by no means the most extreme. On and on it goes until the heart is weary and the mind frustrated to the point of exasperation in trying to cope with and explain such poverty in an "affluent" society.

The Report of the Task Force on Housing and Urban Development, which I had the honour to chair in 1968-69, put the situation more poignantly than I can. It described the urban environment in this way.

> *Here too, is poverty in its rawest and ugliest form. No pretty gardens or painted cottages here to camouflage economic depression. Poverty in the worst areas of the city core is abundantly visible in the decrepit structures which form its housing, the cracked pavements of the streets which are its recreational area, and the rodents which are its wildlife. This poverty you can see – and hear – and taste – and smell. Its residents are not simply families struggling to catch up to the average national income; too often they are people fighting to retain a vestige of human dignity and self-respect. No Task Force impression is more vivid of mind or depressing of spirit than those found amid the blight and slum of Canada's larger cities.*[3]

It is ironic – more than ironic, it is tragic – that in Canada we have had a Senate Committee investigating the causes of poverty at the same time that the government has been pursuing policies that are one of the primary causes of poverty.[4] It makes no sense. It is a case of the left hand not knowing what the right hand is doing. Most tragic of all, the people who are unemployed as a direct result of government policy are those who are least able to fend for themselves. They are the ones with the least education, the least seniority, the least collective strength. They are the disadvantaged who should be the beneficiaries of "liberal" concern rather than the victims of governments' inhumanity.

The elimination of poverty has been one of the elusive goals in the private capital system. It need not be. Certainly a quick look at GNP statistics suggests that the industrialized countries generate enough wealth to support everyone decently. The problem is bad distribution.

Some of the countries I have visited achieved a more just distribution of income than that of Canada and the United States. This is partly because the United States and Canada "enjoy" unemployment levels which are much higher than the average of the industrialized countries.[5] But this fact should not be allowed to obscure the structural problem caused by the inequality between minimum wages and those paid in the large highly capitalized, highly unionized industries.

I do not want to give the impression that nothing has been accomplished. Citing Canadian experience as an example, there has been an enormous change in the income profile of families since 1951.

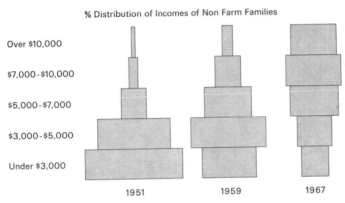

% Distribution of Incomes of Non Farm Families

Over $10,000

$7,000-$10,000

$5,000-$7,000

$3,000-$5,000

Under $3,000

1951   1959   1967

Higher incomes mean that there were as many families earning more than $7,000 a year in 1967 as there had been earning less than $3,000 in 1951.

From *The Financial Post*, April 25, 1970.

This chart is for family income, however, and in some cases the dramatic change has been achieved by the simple expedient of having both husband and wife work. In some cases, this is a desirable arrangement. In other cases, it is impractical and, occasionally, disastrous. Although the chart indicates real progress, it tends to obscure some of the remaining cases of real hardship.

Any figures designed to show how long it would take to bring the incomes of the bottom third of the income scale to reasonably acceptable standards are based on such arbitrary premises and subject to so many variables that I have not bothered to attempt a schedule. What is a reasonable standard? How much of increased production can be directed to increase low incomes? How much has to be retained as capital to increase the productivity of the economy as a whole? There can be wide differences of opinion in judging these questions. One thing is certain, however. Any solution that is economically and politically feasible will take years to implement. This unavoidable slowness makes it imperative that we pursue policies that will, in the long run, bear fruit.

The current conventional solution for poverty is the Guaranteed Annual Wage (G.A.W.). I have just read a number of newspaper articles suggesting that such a scheme should be the next objective of social security policy. The suggestion has been repeated so often – usually by people who have done little, if any, hard thinking about it – that a climate of acceptability has already been created in many circles. I do not agree with the suggestion. Of course, there are a variety of G.A.W. plans. But I have not been impressed by the several versions which have come my way. They pay minimum amounts without a means test. They reduce payments as extra income is earned. While I look forward to seeing other plans, I doubt that this is the solution for the employable poor.

My basic objection is not theoretical. It comes from dozens of case histories illustrating the effects of "disincentive" programs. If, for example the income payment is reduced by 50 cents for every extra dollar of income earned, the recipient considers that he is being taxed at a 50 per cent rate. He may think that the game is just not worth it. I received a letter from a constituent sometime ago making precisely that complaint and drawing exactly that conclusion. He had decided to give up the attempt to earn more. He quit work. The story bears telling only because it is not exceptional.

In the past few years, we Canadians have introduced far too many programmes with built-in disincentives. In each of the ten provinces a married man with two children can earn more tax-paid disposable income by being on welfare than he can by accepting jobs at the lower end of the pay scale. This means that welfare payments are higher than minimum legal wages. As a result, significant numbers of people remain on welfare, not because they enjoy it, but because they would be no better off financially by going to work. In some cases they would be worse off. The logic involved is not difficult. People are not fools: governments occasionally are.

There is another objection to the G.A.W. plan: it will require another addition to our already massive bureaucracy. This means feeding and watering more civil servants. The G.A.W. involves extra cost which has to be borne by everyone, including the people obtaining the benefit. Is there any reason why we should always choose the most complicated and expensive option?

My preference is for the minimum wage solution. I concluded this many years ago on the basis of careful examination of both economic and social considerations. It is true that higher minimum wages would mean higher prices, especially in the service industries. But, I think, no higher than would result from increased taxes and swollen bureaucracy. As a matter of fact, the increase in prices would be a bit less by an amount equal to the brokerage (the real saving due to greater efficiency). Increased prices are inevitable under either system. These are taken into account in the averages discussed elsewhere. There is every reason to choose the option that would have the least effect on prices.

Far more important than this marginal difference in cost – though it should not be dismissed – is the social consideration. One of my basic concerns is with the effect of government policies and programmes on the human spirit. Generally speaking, people are sick of handouts for something that should be theirs as a matter of right. They are sick of welfare, income supplements, subsidized housing and food stamps as an alternative to a decent living wage. They are sick of being studied, pitied, investigated and bullied when all they want is an income that will enable them to keep themselves and their families in human dignity – and to be left alone.

I have long been aware of this deep desire on the part of "the poor." But never had it registered so forcefully on me as it did in the fall of 1968. As Chairman of the Canadian Federal Task Force on Housing and Urban Development, I had the opportunity to visit most of the major urban centres in Canada and to talk directly with hundreds of people about problems of all kinds, but especially about housing and income.[6] Some of the unhappiest people in the country were living in bright new public housing and were "enjoying" very heavy public subsidies. They seemed to have a lot going for them. But something was missing. That something was their freedom and their dignity. Many of the experts have not yet been able to realize this fact. Perhaps they will someday, after many more millions have been squandered.

The poor people we talked to said they wanted adequate earned income. They wanted to make their own decisions. They wanted to set their own priorities. They felt strongly that they knew their own needs better than "big brother" did. They are tired of being watched. They want to be free to make their own mistakes and to learn from doing.

I am not so naive to believe that no one with adequate income is in need of professional help. Of course, there are people who will always need some assistance, but these are a very small minority. Most could manage quite well if they had an adequate steady income. These are the persons whose problems would be basically solved by employment at a living wage. This approach might create some redundancies in the ranks of civil servants and social workers. With enlightened monetary and fiscal policy, however, there should be no difficulty in offering alternative employment.

In the process of readjusting (or adjusting) distribution, it is necessary to look at the relationship of all groups to each other. There is no such thing as perfect distribution. That goal is a will o' the wisp in either private capital or state capital systems. What is necessary is a working arrangement. This does not have to be permanent or rigid. It just has to be a scale to work toward. It can be dynamic and changed from time to time – as inevitably it will be. At the outset, it may be necessary to redress some of the distortions that have been aggravated in the last ten years.

For example, the gap between wages in different industries is far too great. People working for minimum wages, or thereabouts, cannot afford to buy the products of industrial workers. They cannot afford television sets, refrigerators, cars or houses. The graphs on pages 153 and 154 illustrate this point.[7]

The point is not that there are no legitimate differences in wages. There are differences of skill, risk and discomfort among

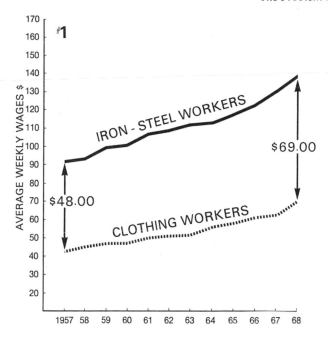

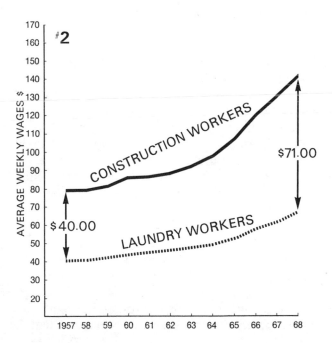

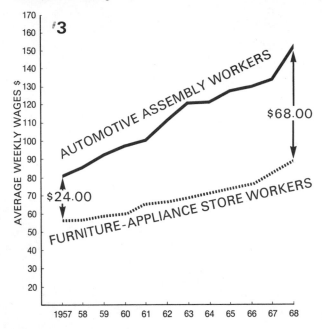

jobs. But there is serious doubt that the differences in wages are in proportion to the differences in jobs. The solution to this problem is primarily a job for labour, but since judgements are subjective, it will be necessary to review them periodically. This process is merely an extension to society at large of the consideration given to relative merit within a plant or industry – difficult, yes, but possible if applied conscientiously.

Once acceptable differentials were set, agreement would be necessary on the time period to achieve them. To move quickly would be unacceptable to the higher paid workers; a slow transition would be unacceptable to those at the bottom of the scale. The ideal would be a dramatic increase at the bottom end of the scale in two or three years and, thereafter, a slower increase over a five to ten year period. The purpose of this is something approaching the social justice we all proclaim.

Once the agreed scale was achieved, the increases would in all cases approximate the average annual increase in output in real terms. It might be necessary to reduce slightly the percentage at the top in favour of the lower groups. For example, and these figures are merely illustrative, if wages in one category were set at $1.50 an hour and another of higher skill at $2.00 an hour, the differential would be 50¢ an hour. If each rate increased by 3 per cent a year for ten years, at the end of the decade the percentage difference would of course be the same but the absolute difference would have increased to 66¢ an hour. It might not be in the public interest to allow indefinite increases in this gap. This is the kind of problem that would require continual review.

I believe that this is essential. The future of our economic system is at stake. The necessary adjustments will not be easy. In the state capital systems, workers have little choice, they do as they are told. In a private capital system with democratic government, basic changes are possible only with the over-whelming support of a majority convinced of the justice and long-range advantages to all. It is an achievable goal.

Notes

1. The Economic Council of Canada, *Fifth Annual Review*, 1968.
2. Trinity Riding in Toronto. Until the last redistribution it was exclusively a workingman's district with many immigrant families from some three dozen different countries. It is still predominantly a workingman's district.
3. *Report of the Task Force on Housing and Urban Development, 1969*, p. 11. Reproduced by permission of Information Canada.
4. At the time of writing (1970).
5. The average rate of unemployment (1958-1966) for Canada was 5.4 per cent, for the U.S. 5.3 per cent. These compare with rates of 1.2 per cent for Germany, 4.0 per cent for Italy, 0.5 per cent for France and 1.7 per cent for the U.K. For a list of unemployment rates of 15 OECD countries see Table 1, Chapter 10, "*The Mathematics of Inflation.*"
6. The two are very directly related.
7. The graphs show only the absolute difference in wages. We should note here the change in relative wages as well. In the case of clothing and iron and steel workers, the relative difference in wages decreases by some 2.5 per cent. In the case of laundry and construction workers, the relative difference increases by 5.5 per cent. In the case of furniture store and auto assembly workers, the relative difference in wages increases by a very considerable 11 per cent.

Chapter **18**

Individual Security
in an Impersonal
Society

By providing full employment at fair wages, you are providing
a guaranteed annual wage for the great majority. There remains
the necessity of providing income for the unemployables, the
deserted and the disabled. It is also necessary to quiet the fears
of unemployment, sickness, disability and old age which haunt
all of us sometime during the course of our lives.

The need for security is innate. A baby needs the comfort-
ing reassurance of a mother's arms. At each stage in our lives,
we need to know that, when we are under attack by forces
strange to us and seemingly beyond our control, we can rely on
someone or something. This fundamental yearning has been
met in various ways – first and foremost, by the family. In
feudal times, the Lord of the Manor accepted some overriding
responsibility for the welfare of his serfs. As the Industrial Revolution progressed and up until the present, society became more
and more impersonal with the consequence that increasing
numbers of people found themselves living, working, suffering
and ultimately dying all alone.

There are, of course, some pleasant exceptions. There are

some business organizations that take an active paternal interest in the welfare of their employees and the employees' families. The Japanese, for example, have their own unique system. In Japan, an employee expects to spend his entire working career with the same company. It is a two-way arrangement. The company can expect the worker to remain in its employ and to provide faithful and worthwhile service while, on the other side, the company is expected to manage its affairs in a way that will provide continuous employment until retirement. Meanwhile, the company takes a direct interest in providing decent housing, sickness and retirement benefits for its employees. The atmosphere of cooperation varies considerably from company to company as you might expect, but is so good generally that you often find union employees singing the company song at a local fair – a most unlikely phenomenon in most countries. No one knows how long the present Japanese system will last; it is generally agreed, however, that the possibility of copying the system in other private capital countries is extremely remote.

Other countries with great mobility of labour are evolving their own security systems. The results, to date, vary considerably but the trend is unmistakable and rational. It is not possible for an individual to provide for every exigency in a modern society. An urban dweller who is ill may be thousands of miles from his family. The family may be completely unaware of his need or in no position to help. There has to be some substitute for the traditional lines of obligation. There has to be some adequate and absolutely reliable protection against the disabling fear of unemployment, sickness, hospitalization, disaster, and even old age.

Assuming an intelligent monetary and fiscal policy, unemployment insurance should be relatively simple and quite inexpensive. This presumes, of course, that it is genuine unemployment insurance and not subject to many of the abuses that have filtered into the Canadian system. It should not include pregnancy insurance, holiday insurance, sabbatical leave insurance, and so on. Of course some of these things are worth insuring. As I have discovered for myself, a sabbatical year is a very interesting, rewarding and useful experience. But it would be tidier to put these under other categories and keep the accounting clear. Unemployment insurance, moreover, should not be supplementary income for seasonal workers who have already earned more than the national average annual income.[1] It should not be an unearned bonanza for one member of a family who is tired of working and whose spouse is employed at a good wage. It should not be paid to people who decide, as a matter of choice, to take a few weeks off between jobs. It should not be paid to people who are retired. Rather, it should be available for indefinite periods to people who cannot obtain a job at a decent minimum wage through no fault of their own — in other words, for those who are unemployed either because the system is not being run properly or due to unusual circumstances. Unemployment insurance should be an ultimate protection for the individual against the incompetence of the establishment.

Sickness and hospitalization insurance are critically important; the kind of plan required, however, is a matter of great controversy. Suggestions, and plans in operation throughout Canada, range from complete government responsibility for the first dollar of expenditure through to genuine insurance for risks beyond the capability of the individual. I do not believe that it is necessary for government to pay the first few dollars, as they do in some plans. I think that genuine insurance for risks beyond the capability of individuals is preferable. It costs less and it requires the government to raise less money through taxation. Furthermore, by giving people the responsibility to make decisions where it is within their competence to do so, you give them a chance to grow. By insuring risks beyond the capability of individuals, you provide them with all the basic protection they require while, at the same time, minimizing "over-consumption." And, finally, by keeping the cost down to a reasonable level you can insure *all* of the unusual risks a person might encounter rather than just some of them. In other words, you can have wider coverage.

There is a Chinese proverb which reads as follows:

Give a man a fish and you will feed him for one day. Teach a man to fish and he may feed himself for a lifetime.

Any drill instructor, mechanic, musician, farmer, teacher, or anyone who has lived a little and learned a little will testify to the wisdom of this saying. People learn by doing. Too much paternalism can be self-defeating. The people who have most developed their skill and decision-making capacity are those who have made a lot of mistakes and learned from those mistakes.

I was born on a farm with innumerable gates. Each gate had a different catch and locking mechanism. Some of them were quite complicated. When I was a boy, my father used to give me the pleasure of opening the gates and he would sit – often for periods that seemed endless to an impatient youth – while I figured out "the combination." Father, of course, could have opened them with a flick of the finger. Eventually, after a frustrating apprenticeship, I could too. Father understood the process of learning and he applied it.

It would be wrong to think that even the wisest and most knowledgeable people reach the stage where they never make mistakes. Even the wisest of bureaucrats make mistakes. A nation of people who learn to be self-reliant will be more imaginative and progressive than people for whom all decisions are made by a select few.

A second reason for applying the insurance principle to health and hospitalization is to minimize over-consumption. In some countries with comprehensive plans, I asked a number of officials about over-consumption. All but two admitted privately – but candidly – that this was a very serious problem. It had resulted in hospital beds being occupied by the insured, but well, and not being available for the sick. It had resulted in a severe rationing problem for doctors' time and an alarming increase in the use of drugs. The two gentlemen who dissented both gave me what I interpreted to be "political" answers. One was press secretary to a senior minister and obviously felt that he could say nothing else.

In support of the thesis on over-consumption, I would like to give three examples. The first of these is from personal experience. At the end of World War II, I bought an insurance policy that was described at the time as a "personal floater policy." It cost $25 a year and was very comprehensive. My first claim against the policy was for a lost slide-rule. The second claim was for a "no-draft car window" which I had broken to gain entry after locking the doors with the keys left in the ignition. The third claim was for a gabardine all-weather coat. Meanwhile, the cost of the policy rose steadily. It went from $25 to $50, then to $75 and finally to $125 a year. At that point, it became too expensive for me and I dropped it largely because the risk it was insuring me against was one I could afford to carry myself. There were other more serious risks that I felt should be insured.

The second example relates to car insurance. Why do most people accept a $25, $50 or $100 deductibility clause in respect to collision insurance? The answer, surely, is the cost. I cannot remember one family car that did not have a scratch, nick or dent of some kind within a few weeks of purchase. Usually these go unnoticed unless someone points them out. Such minor defects are ignored or "stored up" until someone gives the fender a good bash and then everything is repaired at once. Repairs are necessary only when the car's performance is affected. One hundred per cent prepaid insurance fails by encouraging needless repairs. It seems "free." Try it and see for yourself.

The third example of over-consumption applies to first-class air travel. People who would normally have one drink before dinner and perhaps a glass of wine with dinner, can be persuaded to take two drinks before dinner, a little white wine with the lobster, a little red wine with the steak, a glass of port or a liqueur after dinner and perhaps even a glass of champagne for good measure. They may also eat far more than they normally would. Why? Because it seems free! It's included in the price of the ticket. To say no to anything is to miss something you are entitled to because you have already paid for it. The fact that you do not *need* to eat or drink that much does not matter. Nor does it matter that you wouldn't pay for such consumption à la carte. The busy traveller may have the willpower to say no. But most casual travellers find the "availability" irresistible.

Over-consumption diverts scarce resources from people in need. It also involves vast expenditures for goods and services that people would happily do without if they could see the connection with their own pocketbook.

A final justification for limited liability health insurance is that it finances wider coverage. Most existing plans omit something of importance: dental care, plastic surgery, sometimes prosthetic services, or it may be the extra cost of sending a child who needs special care or training to a distant school. By using the insurance principle it would be possible, for a reasonable premium, to compensate such extraordinary expenditures related to the physical or mental health of the individual.

During the debate on medicare in Canada, one suggestion was that the individual carry his own risk for 2 per cent of his income. People with no income would be completely covered. People earning $3,000 a year would be responsible for the first $60 of expenditure. Those earning $30,000 annually would pay the first $600. To provide full coverage for the special areas I have mentioned might require 3 per cent individual liability. These figures are merely illustrative. It is the principle that is important. People should buy their own aspirin or bandaids in the normal course. At the same time, they should be fully covered for all risks which they, as individuals, cannot meet. In this way the maximum of services would be available to the greatest number in real need. Risk sharing is the name of the game.

Disability Allowance

There are many degrees of disability, ranging from total to very slight. Many disabled persons fall into one of the two classes of unemployables or semi-unemployables. They should be guaranteed some income as a matter of right. For a person who is totally disabled, the amount should be enough to live on – in effect, a guaranteed annual income. For the partially disabled, an award should be made which, taken together with a reasonable expectation of income from other sources, would be sufficient to keep them comfortably. These partial awards should be subject to review upward at any time in the event of changing circumstances. They should be subject to revision downward only at stated intervals, maybe once every five years. There should be no disincentive to initiative and gainful employment.

It might be necessary to exempt partially disabled persons from minimum wage laws so they can make their own market. That is an administrative detail. The important principles are these: that we err on the side of generosity and that we encourage initiative. These are not based on the economics of maximum output but rather on a recognition of two rights: the right to receive and the right to give.

Desertion Allowance

The one-parent family is the other case where some form of guaranteed annual income is required. No single solution will meet all cases. Where young and school-age children are involved, some parents prefer to devote their full attention to them. Others would prefer to have daycare centres for the children in order to permit the parent to work. Either option should be feasible. Whether society has a preference for one solution over the other is a moot point. Without getting lost in that never-never land of sociology and psychology, may I suggest that, at least, there should be no social or financial pressure exerted on mothers to abandon the full-time care of their children. In any event, and under either option, it should be understood that the income available will be adequate to keep parent and children decently, including adequate food, clothing and shelter. This should be accomplished without resort to charity or handouts in the traditional sense and without too much bureaucratic supervision. This is a bit tricky in view of the benefits bestowed on commonlaw relationships by the people who write our tax laws.[2] However, such law is subject to change. Some day they may give the married couple, who accept legal responsibility for raising their children, an even break.

Old Age Pensioners

Providing for old age is not really an insurance problem. It is a universal savings problem. It requires for its solution either a funded retirement plan or the payment of pensions from current income. The latter is the current vogue but I cast my long-range vote for funded plans. I have several good reasons.

First of all, based on the Canadian experience, it will help to make politicians more honest. (Whether it will be enough to get them to heaven I don't know, but it should take some of the heat off.) In 1949, we introduced a non-contributory, non-funded universal Old Age pension plan. It was clearly stated at the time that it was to be a supplement to private savings. Little by little, through the years, the politicians and the press – in this case, it is difficult to decide which is the devil and which the deep blue sea – have persuaded first the Canadian people and then themselves that it was intended to be an adequate retirement allowance. The fact that it is not is assumed to be the politicians' calloused view of what old people need, or should have, to live in their old age.

This problem is more than just a generational difference between those who pay and those who receive. It is symptomatic of a total lack of understanding of our economic system, how it works, and its limitations. Politicians and journalists stumble over each other raising bids for the next increase. They never stop to think or to say that a general increase may mean, for example, selling more Canadian assets to foreigners. In any case, it means an increase in current expenditure at the cost of savings, with the result of a slower growth rate in the economy. This in turn means less preparation for the "next round" and probably fewer jobs for young people entering the labour force. And because the scheme is universal, many of the people for whom this sacrifice is made do not need the extra money. For the ones who do, those with no private savings at all, it is not adequate. To cure the situation in the short run requires the re-introduction of some kind of needs test so that the people who get the extra money are the ones who really require it. The longer-run solution requires an entirely different kind of system – one that is collected, accounted for, and administered without too much help from the politicians. Their record of irresponsibility in these matters is incredible.

A system that escapes the whims of politics and politicians to the maximum extent should have the following characteristics: it should be universal, fully vesting and fully portable. In other words, each person's pension should be accounted separately from day one. His contribution and that of his employer should be invested by the approved investment agency of his choice. The problem of losing benefits when changing jobs would no longer exist. A person could switch from industry to government, to academic life and back again without losing his accumulated pension rights. He would enjoy a freedom born of true portability.

He would also contribute to the growth of his country through the ownership of capital goods. At least part of his savings would be invested in equities, subject to proper safeguards, making him a direct beneficiary of the economic well being of the private capital system.

There would be complete flexibility at retirement. An annuity could be purchased at any age; the later the retirement age, the greater the annuity. Each plan could be tailored to the needs of the individual or his survivor. There would be no question of ownership and, consequently, no suggestion that entitlement would cease if the recipient moved to another country. It would be his pension to enjoy and to spend where and when he pleased.

The extra capital formation would also benefit any developing nation. This would be particularly important in underdeveloped countries but it would apply, as well, in countries like Canada which is a net importer of capital. The benefits would be both personal and national.

The justification for the universality of the scheme is related to our kind of society. As discussed earlier, the old chain of responsibility involving family and community is breaking down. At the same time, there is no way that society at large can ignore the need of any aged individual. It becomes a matter of equity, then, that each of us make a contribution to our own retirement. Each of us would expect benefits. The standard of life expected would be related to our accustomed life style. This would be fair, if the contributions had been proportionate. Only in the most unusual circumstance would it be necessary to supplement a benefit from general tax revenues. Adequate pensions would be available to all citizens in accordance with a plan made for each of them.

I am sure someone will exclaim "cradle to the grave security." Exactly! What we are looking for is a lifelong substitute for the responsibility which used to reside exclusively with the family or, failing that, with the Lord of the Manor. But cradle to grave security is not the same as cradle to grave paternalism. It is a world apart. The system I am talking about lets individuals run their own lives to the maximum extent possible while providing something every high-wire act should have but sometimes neglects: a life-saving net in case of accident so as to keep people from smashing their lives irretrievably.

The key to maximum freedom with maximum security is full employment at fair wages. It is the cornerstone upon which the superstructure is built.

Notes

1. One example will illustrate. A bulldozer operator in Northern Saskatchewan earned $14,000 in seven months and then drew unemployment insurance all winter.
2. The Canadian situation.

Chapter **19**

The Leisure Myth
and the
Quality of Life

Some months ago I read a newspaper article quoting a professor from the University of Windsor to the effect that soon it would be possible to adopt the 20-hour week. I must admit that I was both angry and disturbed by what I read. Angry to note such a total lack of understanding of economics by someone who presumably should know better. Disturbed because the article reinforced the myth that the work week can be substantially reduced without a reduction in take-home pay (in real terms) and without undermining our attack on the high priority problems to which we pay lip service such as poverty, urban renewal, housing and pollution control. Certainly there are options available to us but we cannot exercise them all in the short term. We must still make choices.

I have discussed the problem of poverty in a previous chapter. The present discussion turns to other tasks on the liberal agenda. But let us keep two things in mind: poverty is still the major obstacle to the qualities of life, and poverty is intertwined with the other obstacles.

Urban Renewal

A substantial portion of the higher incomes generated by better economic performance would be spent for improved shelter. Accommodation would be improved. While this might reduce pressure for public spending in some areas, such as public housing, it would tend to increase the pressure for other improvements in the public sector such as roads, parks and schools. Rehabilitated houses require rehabilitated streets and neighbourhoods. In many cases it would make sense to install new sewer, water, gas and hydro lines before repaving the streets. (Most city works departments I've known prefer doing it the other way around.) There are thousands of miles of inadequate and obsolete sewers in our great cities. There are miles of unsafe gas mains. Some of the water distribution systems are inadequate, others almost rusted out.

Some public buildings, too, are in urgent need of repair or replacement. There are ancient schools that are pure firetraps. Our children should not suffer that kind of risk. There are jails so dark and dank and horrible that the psychological effects on young and first offenders are incalculable (though predictable in their results). And so it is with other institutions as well. One of my unforgettable experiences was visiting an institution for the mentally ill with a choir of which I was a member. The indelible impression I got from this and other visits was that anyone who was not sick of mind and heart at the time of admission soon would be when confined in such weary soul-destroying quarters.

The list of urgent improvements necessary in public facilities is a long and expensive one. I would not attempt to put a price tag on these. The price would vary with individual criteria. To give you a general idea of the order of magnitude, I would like to quote briefly from an article which appeared in *U.S. News and World Report* in the fall of 1966:

When Robert F. Kennedy, New York Senator, added up suggested costs of federal aid for cities, he concluded that if figures for major cities were extended to all, the total for the next 10 years would be 1.1 trillion dollars.[1]

The National Planning Association predicts that 2.1 trillion dollars will be necessary to make American cities "viable."[2]

I think that it is probably impossible to put a price tag on what it is going to cost to save the cities. Nevertheless, I have no quarrel with the order of magnitude of these estimates. It is difficult to appear before a Senate sub-committee and not produce some estimate of what has to be done. These educated guesses are sufficient to underline the seriousness of the problem at the early stages of policy formulation.

After a few months as Federal Minister in charge of Housing and then as Chairman of the Task Force on Housing and Urban Development, I came to the conclusion that the problems of Canadian cities were not very different from those of our American neighbours. Some of our cities are not quite as old and therefore we have a slight time advantage – if we use it. Looking to the future, however, ours is just a smaller version of the American urban crisis.

Cities in other countries are not immune. In the course of my research for this book, I had the pleasure of visiting quite a few large cities[3] in a number of countries. Some obviously required a great deal more rehabilitation than others. But there was not one that did not need a lot of money to improve or just to maintain its quality of life.

The point of the argument is simply that huge amounts of money and human effort must be spent over the next several decades. In some cases, this may improve cities. In others, it may only maintain an existing level of tolerance. In either case, our choice is extremely limited. Either we make the effort or we face, quite literally, a hell on earth.

Housing

As already indicated, one direct consequence of higher incomes should be a demand for better shelter. This should prove true both for employables and unemployables, assuming that income is raised to the level where they can afford the basic necessities. The job to be done in providing adequate shelter for everyone is staggering.

The standard of housing in Canada is probably as good as in any country in the world and it is better than most. Yet as a member of the Task Force on Housing, I saw first-hand the wretched conditions under which too many of our fellow-countrymen live – rat-infested hovels unfit for human habitation; shacks and shanties of indescribable shape and variety, which most farmers would have considered unfit for animals; electric wiring and unprotected stoves that would terrify anyone with even a slight respect for fire and its tragic consequences; people living in basements and attics and tents and barracks; broken windows, cracked plaster and bad plumbing. In short, the shelter was not protective of life but a hazard to it. It was after seeing this squalor amidst affluence that the Task Force concluded: "Every Canadian should be entitled to clean, warm shelter as a matter of basic human right."

The housing problem is not unique to Canada. It is worldwide. The requirements in the United States are similar. There, too, millions of people are living in substandard, subhuman conditions. It is a cancer in the national body made all the more deadly by the contrast with what exists for the affluent and what is possible. There is no solution for the violence of minority groups that does not include jobs and decent housing for all.

In Stockholm, there is an acute physical shortage of accommodation. Long under government control, the supply is not adequate for the demand. I learned that there was about an eight-year waiting period for one of the subsidized Stockholm apartments. Young people who registered at age eighteen could expect their names to come to the top of the list at about age 26. Pregnancy and other considerations are taken into account but one wonders whether even the sex mores are not affected by the lack of accommodation.

I could list other countries I have visited which have housing problems, but it is not necessary. Generalizations are dangerous in any area, including housing, but it is safe to say that in most countries a tremendous effort and vast expenditures are required to provide everyone with some objective standard of "clean warm shelter."

Urban Transportation

Many governments are making a valiant effort to encourage industry to locate in small centres. It is a losing battle. The migration to the big cities is a worldwide phenomenon. This is partly a function of the technological revolution in agriculture.

A century ago, the great majority of our population was engaged in agriculture. Today it is a steadily diminishing minority. The forces that attract people to the great cities are complex but it was Constantine Doxiades, the noted Greek city planner who summed them up as "the maximization of contact with the minimum of effort." There are more job opportunities in the big cities. There is a greater variety of schools and educational opportunities. The range of cultural activities and attractions is greatest there. Whether you seek variety in food, entertainment, employment, education, religion or any other pursuit, you will find it in a big city. In other words, the city is where the action is.

The inflow of new citizens and seemingly uncontrolled growth, however, has created problems of great magnitude. Not the least of these is transportation. The downtown streets of many great cities were "designed" in the horse-and-buggy age. They have been adapted for the automobile age – but never successfully. The technological revolution caused by the car has changed our whole life style but we have not yet mastered the change. As usual, the changes in our thinking and institutions necessary to adjust to the world of the automobile lag behind the impact of the technology itself. Consequently, we still see traffic engineers trying to redesign big cities around the automobile – an impossible task.

In large cities it is impossible for the great mass of people to move quickly and comfortably by automobile. It is mathematically absurd to put 1.3 persons into 120 square feet of machine and move thousands of these machines from the sprawling suburbs into the small core city. Horses made the trip in 1890 faster than the machines make it in 1971. This is what Mark Twain meant by "all the modern inconveniences."

The only solution is a fully integrated public transportation system. I would not attempt to describe what the system should look like. This is a job for the experts and they are only beginning to examine the range of alternatives. I fully appreciate the magnitude of the problems they face. Our cities were not designed for public transportation systems and, consequently, you seldom, if ever, find the right mix of densities required to support a system and to minimize the travel time in relation to cost. Average speeds are limited by comfortable rates of acceleration and deceleration. The distance between stations is critical if one is talking about rapid transit. There are many unanswered questions. For example, is it necessary for local trains to run on the same track as the express trains?

These problems are soluble. Integrated transportation can work – EXPO 67 proved it. Its system was not as fully integrated as originally planned but it did prove that the combination of rapid transit, Expo express, minirail and battery car could move hundreds of thousands of people into, around and out of the site in reasonable comfort. Given an adequate research programme and enough money for some trial and error application, systems could be developed that would be much superior to anything we now know. The design and redesign of cities would be part of the total enquiry. The transportation system and the city system it serves have to be compatible – integral parts of a total system. If they are, the benefits will be comfort, convenience, low-cost and safety, not to mention clean air. The design, development and installation of a system to meet these criteria will involve the expenditure of vast amounts of energy and effort and, yes, money.

Pollution Control

When discussing the importance of integrated public transportation systems, I concentrated on the obvious potential benefits in speed, comfort, convenience and cost and deliberately glossed over the dividends available from noise and air pollution control. I want to emphasize that importance in this section.

The automobile is one of the worst polluters of the urban environment. It spews its noxious gases relentlessly into the urban air. It is at its worst when idling. The greater the traffic strangulation, the slower the average speed, the greater the pollution. The net effect has reached alarming levels and has become a matter of major concern to "people who care." No doubt "cleaner" cars can and will be built. The object, however, is to eliminate as far as possible the air pollution and noise pollution effects of urban transportation. It would appear that something less noxious than the internal combustion engine is necessary. And it is clear this must be a matter of urgent priority!

The automobile, although a major contributor, is not the only polluter of the urban scene. Factories, power plants, furnaces, airplanes, sewers and incinerators play their part. The list is long and formidable. In talking about pollution, the subject sometimes seems abstract and remote, a problem affecting other people in other places. But recently it became a very tangible and personal thing for me and my family.

We live in a bungalow on the Rideau River in Ottawa South. It is a beautiful location and central to everything in Ottawa. About two hundred yards down the street is Brighton Beach. It is one of the reasons we chose our house. We thought, and it proved to be true, that it would be nice to enjoy a quick dip before dinner on a hot summer's evening or before lunch on the weekend when the pressure of work is not quite so great. Two years ago the beach was closed because raw sewage was dumped into the river from an overloaded sewer system in Nepean township. A year ago, everyone had their fingers crossed because the folks at Smiths Falls, a bit further upstream were using the river as an open ditch for untreated effluent. "Our" river is polluted.

There are other examples. On days when the wind is from the east, the air is heavy with sulphur dioxide from the E.B. Eddy Company, just across the big Ottawa River. The plant is on the Quebec side of the river and under our somewhat feeble Constitution the pollution from its smokestack is deemed to be a provincial responsibility. I guess the wind is not supposed to blow from the east, but sometimes it does, and when it does we just have to wait for the wind to change and the stench to disappear.

Even then, it is not as bad as the smell we were subjected to the night the Task Force on Housing visited Windsor, Ontario. After a long day of formal hearings, we retired to the Holiday Inn for the night. The Inn is right on the water and you can step out on your balcony and breathe deeply and enjoy the night skyline of Detroit. But you breathe deeply at your own risk. In joyful anticipation, we threw open the balcony doors and inhaled. The gasps were audible. The air was sick. After a quick look and with almost indecent haste, it was back inside to the protection of closed doors and windows. The contaminated air was coming south across the international boundary. Once again the winds were indifferent to politics.

Toronto, Hamilton, Detroit, Los Angeles and Tokyo, like many of their sister cities, are members of the club. Twice in recent weeks, the provincially-owned Thermal Electric plant in Toronto was shut down temporarily because the pollution count exceeded acceptable levels. Twice in recent weeks when travelling through Hamilton on my way to and from the family farm, the air was saturated with the polluted stench from the Steel Company of Canada stacks.

And was it last summer or the summer before that a doctor friend jumped into my favourite lake, Muskoka, and gashed his foot badly on a broken bottle that some half-wit had thrown there? The urge to kill! At the summer's end when the lake was quiet, I stayed to rest for a few days and to do a bit of fishing. Although I am not terribly fond of fish, I can't resist a fresh fried bass that I have hooked myself. The fish were good but a couple of weeks later the Provincial Government announced that all the bass in the lake were contaminated with DDT and not fit for human consumption. That is personal enough for me!

The list is long and growing longer. The Economic Council of Canada[4] reports that seventeen Canadian water basins are significantly affected by pollution; seven of our major cities dump 90 per cent or more of their raw sewage directly into rivers or the sea. Twelve Ontario cities fail to meet a single objective standard for air pollution. Again Canada is not unique in its offence. Most other industrialized countries I have visited have similar situations sadly in need of attention.

The Quality of Life

All of these ingredients can be tossed in one salad entitled "The Quality of Life." Poverty, urban blight, inadequate and substandard housing, outdated transportation and noxious pollution have no place in a good salad. Their elimination or improvement, is not just a matter of taste but is in some cases a matter of life itself. Many people have died as a result of pollution. Countless others have been affected to a degree as yet unmeasured. Other people have died spiritually from the crushing burden of rejection and poverty associated with urban slums.

But these things need not be. The problems are formidable, but the tools to cope with them are unprecedented in human history. The range of knowledge is staggering. All we have to do is apply it. Our ability to analyze and solve problems is beyond description. Could one sit down and write a simple yet comprehensive account of the incredible teamwork involved in the Apollo moon missions? Would it be easy to describe the complex systems and sub-systems which harmonized in a moving, thrilling exhibition of "technique"?

Apollo flights taught us what can be done when we join organization and technology – when we harness them together. Unfortunately, it did not prove that we have the common sense to apply the same "technique" to other, and perhaps even more important, problems. I believe that if we chose to apply the same priority and brain power to the solution of our economic and environmental problems we could achieve equally spectacular results.

If time and space permitted, I would be tempted to describe in some detail the kind of urban environment that I believe to be possible. That will have to wait for another occasion. I will content myself with a declaration that we can build and rebuild urban centres in a way that will make it possible for everyone to enjoy clean, warm shelter; to breathe clean air; to swim in unpolluted waters; to move with relative comfort and to see the sun.

Regrettably, no magic wand will do it. It requires thought and dedication and work. Call the effort work, or translate it into money, it all adds up to the same thing. There is much to be done but we have the means if we have the will. Personally I think we must. That is the reason I think the leisure problem, now, is just a myth. The problem for my generation, and probably that of my children too, is to eliminate poverty, blight, pollution and ugliness to the maximum extent possible. Then, if a future generation is faced with the "problem" of more leisure time, they will be able to "relax" in a tolerable world.

Notes

1. "A Trillion Dollars to Save The Cities," *U.S. News and World Report*, October 3, 1966, p. 73.
2. *Ibid.*
3. Amsterdam, Belgrade, Budapest, Cologne, Copenhagen, Frankfurt, Helsinki, Hong Kong, Kiev, London, Manchester, Moscow, Oslo, Prague, Singapore, Stockholm, Sydney, Tokyo and Warsaw.
4. Economic Council of Canada, *Sixth Annual Review*, Sept. 1969, pp. 43-46.

Chapter **20**

Rich Nations
and Poor Nations

To the ancient class system within nations has been added – in the past one hundred years or so – a class system among nations. There are today rich nations and poor nations. There are nations whose per-capita income is thousands of dollars and there are nations whose per-capita income is a few hundreds of dollars. There are nations whose people now enjoy or expect soon to enjoy decent education, health and security. And there are nations whose people suffer overwhelming deprivation, sickness, illiteracy and early death. The rich nations are not uniformly rich. There are poor, sometimes shocking numbers of poor, within them, but the notion of what one may expect or demand is affluent beyond the dreams of most of the world's people. The poor nations are not uniformly poor. There are pockets of great wealth and luxury within them. There are also cultural and social values that the rich occasionally envy. All this notwithstanding, however, there *are* rich nations and poor nations.

Canadians are members of a rich nation. We nurse our modern neuroses and speculate about a future of leisure. But is it reasonable to so worry about what we can do with ourselves in such a world? Is it not time that the notion of leisure face the facts of poverty and need?

There is still loose in the rich nations the silly notion that our obligation to the poor nations is a moral luxury, a kind of modern charity. The concept of charity rests on the supposition that there are separate worlds with only an occasional surplus of generosity crossing the gap. We "give" out of the goodness of our heart. This is dangerous nonsense – for two reasons. First, it ignores that our "giving" has usually been connected to our "receiving." We, the rich, have played a major role in the making of poor nations. Second, it ignores that we are in the midst of a single inter-connected world on the make. The clichés about East and West, rich and poor, traditional and modern are pathetically dated. We are all changing together. There are differences but they are differences of an essential similarity. There are national and cultural parochialisms but they all face the same basic question. How can we survive together? The rest is mainly quaint nonsense from the "good old days."

It is time to act. Our reasons may vary from moral outrage that the poor should not suffer their lot to a shrewd fear that they will not suffer it. In the crudest terms of self interest it is now absurd to imagine that equal doses of force and fatalism will keep the poor quiet.

Yet it is one thing to eliminate nonsense and quite another to initiate action. What to do? One ancient solution is to take from the rich and give to the poor. This faces two objections. The rich do not like it and, more to the point, it does not work. Donations create needs but not capacities. What is required is for the poor to learn toughness and skills.

This is simply said but not so easily done. The problem is not a new one. "For every one that hath shall be given and he shall have abundance: but from him that hath not shall be taken away even that which he hath".[1] Poverty is a habit and like all habits it is self-reinforcing.

Men and women were sick because they were poor; they became poorer because they were sick and sicker because they were poorer.[2]

The task of opening these vicious circles belongs to the poor themselves. It is the poor nations that must supply the basic energy necessary to growth. But it is obvious that we, the rich, have an impact on the process. We cannot destroy it or achieve it. But we can retard or encourage it. How?

First, there is the matter of expectations. There are still many people – some of them well intentioned – who think that this great change can be a quiet and happy affair; that it can be an affair at which the rich nations are the honoured and comforted guests. One does not have to worship turmoil to see the naivete of this view. George III did not like the American Revolution. Louis XVI is reported to have been disturbed by the French Revolution. It would be curious if the affluent liked all aspects of the current discontent. It is bound to be disquieting. This does not mean that we should welcome turmoil and conflict. It does mean that if we insist on seeing change and discontent solely as a devious plot, we are likely to have more rather than less of it. The poor nations are in the process of transformation. It is essential that they also transform their relations with us. If we mean that they must be tough then we must expect that they will be tough with us. We will be tough enough with them.

Second, there is the matter of international trade. Almost all authorities are in agreement that export-import performance is a crucial factor in development.

The growth rates of individual developing countries since 1950 correlate better with their export performance than with any other single economic indicator. If the expansion of world trade were to flag, the development effort would undoubtedly be retarded.[3]

The reason for this is simple. A favourable balance of trade is a precious source of capital for these countries. Unfortunately, the balance is often unfavourable.

The terms of international trade often run against the poor nations. This is partly a matter of commodity composition. Of the nine countries listed in Gunnar Myrdal's study of Asia, "five are one commodity exporters. That is, more than 50% of the value of their exports is accounted for by one commodity."[4] Moreover these commodities are mainly primary items such as rice, jute, rubber, sugar and tea. Demand for them either grows slowly as income increases in the wealthy countries or it is at the mercy of substitutes.

It is obviously essential that these economies diversify. This is made difficult by the restrictive trade policies of the rich nations. Tariffs and quotas often exist in precisely those areas where the under-developed nations can exploit comparative advantages. Excluding petroleum products, base metals and ships (which have been "exported" to developed countries for repairs), no less than 30 per cent of manufactured goods are subject to quantitative restrictions. Cotton textiles and clothing and processed foodstuffs are subject to such restrictions in most wealthy countries. In addition, a number impose restrictions on non-cotton textiles, leather and leather articles, footwear, dyestuffs, glass and glassware.[5]

There has been some progress in liberalizing trade but major obstacles remain. In Canada, for example, the Department of Trade and Commerce has been under considerable pressure from textile interests to provide protective legislation, including import surcharges. Magsoud Khan, Trade Commissioner for Pakistan, criticized the proposed special designation of a "low-cost import group:"

It's very bad, you know, coining words like this . . . we beat you . . . Instead of accepting your defeat, you say 'Oh it's a low cost industry, . . . I'm suggesting you are only subsidizing your labour. You have high wages and low productivity . . . We are in a position to compete in the foreign market. We are efficient . . . Canadians should recognize defeated industries. They must die.[6]

It is far easier to accept such deaths if they are not accompanied – as they are in Canada – by massive unemployment. Sane domestic policy is obviously essential to the rationalization of world trade.

Besides international trade, there are two other possible outside sources of development capital. These are private investment and "foreign aid." First, a word about private investment. While it has been sizeable it has not been growing rapidly.[7] There are reasons for this. Many developing countries view the private investor as a ghost from the colonial era. In some cases, he behaves as if he were; consequently he is often surrounded with restrictions that escalate the already high risks. But even if light and sweet reason prevailed, private investment would not be an adequate source of development capital. What is required is long-term capital on favourable terms. Only in this way can developing nations plan with some assurance.

At this point, the most maligned and praised of modern enterprises – foreign aid – enters the picture. In recent days its critics have held the floor. They keep asking whether aid pays. They are joined in this questioning by more than a few of the recipients. The doubts stem from the fact that development is a very complex business. It is hard to control.

Economic development is a fickle process; it destroys old habits and attitudes toward life, even as it creates the wherewithal for a better material life; it creates human desires often too much faster than it provides for the means of its gratification; its one continual and overriding requirement is change . . .[8]

The search for a formula that would provide some guarantees to the lending nations, at the same time supplying aid of a kind and quantity that is relevant to development needs is certainly not being abandoned. On the contrary, we may be seeing the emergence of a new stage of development assistance in the form of such institutions as the World Bank, and the Asia Development Bank, which attempt to combine hard project analysis with maximum sensitivity to the needs and apprehensions of the developing countries. To function, however, they require some assurance of long-range capital funds.

One proposal that I strongly endorse is the idea of a guaranteed capital contribution from the rich nations. This is a kind of international income tax.

. . . in a statement adopted at a meeting of the World Council of Churches and circulated to all United Nations delegations [it was] stated that if contributing countries could divert at least 1% of their national income to grants and concessional loans the international picture would be much more hopeful.[9]

This target was subsequently endorsed by the United Nations, though it was amended to include all resource transfers both private and governmental.

Even granting the amendment, performance thus far has

been disappointing. Overall performance has been on the decline in recent years. The Canadian contribution, while on the increase, still ranked last among O.E.C.D. countries in 1968.[10] In the case of official development assistance as a percentage of GNP, Canada ranked ninth (along with Sweden) out of a total of 15 O.E.C.D. countries.[11] On the other hand, Canada is one of only five countries to have recognized officially the 1 per cent target and to be planning to reach that goal by 1975.[12] Just how hard that planning is remains to be seen.

One can recite the facts. Perhaps the recital will do no good. We can remain indifferent for some time yet. But the time is rapidly approaching when we will have to grow up. Privilege is badly distributed in this world. "We" know it. "They" know it. We'd better do something about it.

Notes

1. Matthew 25:29.
2. C.E.A. Winslow, "The Cost of Sickness and the Price of Health," quoted in Gunnar Myrdal, *Rich Lands and Poor: The Road to World Prosperity*, (New York: Harper & Row, 1957), p. 11. This idea of the vicious circle or "cumulative causation" runs as a theme throughout Myrdal's work. It was applied to American race relations in *An American Dilemma* and to Asian poverty in *Asian Drama*.
3. Commission on International Development (Lester Pearson, Chairman), *Partners in Development*, (New York: Praeger, 1969), p. 141.
4. Gunnar Myrdal, *Asian Drama: An Inquiry into the Poverty of Nations*, (New York: Pantheon, 1968), Vol. I, p. 586.
5. *Partners in Development*, pp. 70-71.
6. Quoted in the *Globe and Mail*, August 26, 1970, p. B-2.
7. *Partners in Development*, p. 100.
8. Eugene Black (former President of the World Bank), *The Diplomacy of Economic Development*, quoted in Herbert Feis, *Foreign Aid and Foreign Policy*, (New York: St. Martin's Press, 1964), p. 68.
9. *Partners in Development*, p. 144.
10. Resource flow from Canada to the developing areas as a percentage of Canadian GNP was .39 in 1960, .44 in 1967 and .49 in 1968. By comparison, the corresponding figures for the United States were .75, .69 and .65; for Sweden, .37, .50 and .50; for Japan .58, .69 and .74. See Table 7-2, *Partners in Development*, p. 145.
11. *Ibid.*, Table 7-5, p. 150.
12. The other four countries are Sweden, Norway, Denmark and The Netherlands.

PART FIVE

Liberal Conclusions

Chapter 21

The Range of Choice

It is not my purpose to say that the right solution for man is to work harder and produce more "things" for public and private consumption. Nor, on the other hand, that we should shorten the hours of work and put less emphasis on production of goods and services. I am entitled to an opinion both as an individual and as a public person. As I have already indicated, there are urgent problems to solve before we opt for much more free time. If we want to eliminate poverty and injustice and provide some real quality of life, particularly in the urban centres, much remains to be done. The fight for real progress in these areas will continue and, I hope, produce results, but the real purpose of developing more efficient mechanics of economic management is to broaden the range of choice for individuals, for unions and for societies. An improved system will make private capital attractive in comparison with other systems. Much of the attraction will reside in the broad range of options available to individuals and groups within the free society.

In *The Affluent Society*,[1] Professor John Kenneth Galbraith delightfully debunked much of the "conventional wisdom" of the day. The time has come, he states, when our basic economic needs as individuals have been sufficiently satisfied, but our public needs, those things we use in common such as public parks and recreational facilities, are not adequately provided for.

If one defines the conventional wisdom as an idea which is automatically, and often unthinkingly, accepted and repeated as factual by public experts, politicians, educators and newspaper columnists, then Galbraith's famous "private affluence amidst public squalor" became overnight, as if by magic, a new conventional wisdom. I have seldom heard it challenged.

For the sake of discussion, may I suggest that Galbraith's contention is a dangerous over-generalization. From the day *The Affluent Society* was written until this day, a large proportion of my constituents have lived in private squalor amidst public affluence. A casual inspection will reveal their desperate circumstances. It is not difficult to catalogue the "things" on their priority lists – new furnaces, new clothes, cars that they can afford to maintain, stoves, washing machines, and so on. The list is long; the need is great. Although I speak here of the requirements of those who elect me, I know that there are thousands of people in like circumstances in every big city. Yet, not far away is the public affluence. In my adopted city of Toronto, there is a strikingly beautiful new city hall. There is an Ontario Science Centre with magic attraction for the young and the young-at-heart. In Tokyo, an opulent Bank of Japan building stands as a monument to the new prosperity. In every city, there are great airports with richly-appointed terminal facilities. These seem essential to some of us but they are well beyond the means of the people I am most concerned about. There are super-highways, with their nightmarish spider web interchanges costing countless millions in dollars (and countless thousands in lives) for the convenience of some. These too are unavailable to the poor who cannot afford cars maintained to acceptable safety standards. I could fill a chapter with well-known examples. No doubt you can fill your own chapter. Visit the three or four nicest buildings in your city and then ask the Superintendent of Works, or Planning, where to find a rundown area of substandard houses. Take a look and make a mental list of the "things" required to provide a standard which *you*, would find acceptable. If your reaction is like mine, you will find the experience quite educational.

I do not want to give the impression that I am against modern architecture or interesting scientific exhibits. It is perspective I am seeking. "public squalor amidst private affluence" is only part of the story; so is "public affluence amidst private squalor." It is more precise to say "some public squalor (lack of parks and transportation facilities, etc.) and some private squalor (slums, poverty) amidst some public affluence and some private affluence." The generalizations must be qualified to give a complete picture. The river with an average depth of two inches is dangerously simple.

Professor Galbraith is also in danger of contributing to simple-mindedness in parts of his later book, *The New Industrial State*.[2] He faithfully records, and in the process lends powerful impetus to, the prevailing attitude of his class. "Alienation has been evident," he says, "among youth." It has manifested itself in rejection of conventional attitudes on work, career, clothing and foreign policy. But this unease is not confined to youth. It has been widespread in the educational and scientific estate. And it has invaded, even, the great philanthropic foundations where it has led to grants to groups duly constituted to re-examine the purposes of the society."

The people Galbraith speaks of have much in common. They can hold the new conventional wisdom and be contemptuous of "things" because they do not really need anything. Students travel wearing jeans and sleeping in the fields or in youth hostels. So what? They are strong and resilient. They do travel widely thanks to machines created by the industrial system. You can see them in Europe, or Florida, or Hawaii, or just about anywhere. They may have little money and tattered clothes, but they get around on a grand scale. They know that they can forsake their wanderings and join the "establishment" any time they choose. They have brains and they have education. Those two together spell security. Not the security of money in the bank, but a more reliable security, assuming good health, which is the ability to enter the labour force almost any time and almost anywhere and to be well compensated for any contribution. Of course, there may be a temporary surplus in a particular discipline, but this will pass. In the long run, educated young people have it made, and they know it. They are in a comfortable position from which to philosophize.

The "educational and scientific estate" is similarly blessed. They have security too, perhaps too much. Tenure makes it difficult to remove the most incompetent teacher from his post. Most members of the academic and scientific worlds are well provided with life's basic necessities. Although salaries are not exorbitant, they are ample for food, clothing, shelter, recreation, etc. A little moonlighting or a fellowship of some sort provides variety and travel. The members of the educational and scientific estate appear to have the best trade-off of cash income and free time of any group in society. In other words, like the college students, they are privileged. They have everything they need, can get anything they really want and can afford to be contemptuous of "things", and of the system which produces them.

The members of the educational and scientific estate have the right to think as they please, as do other groups in a free society. I have only two requests to make of them. First, that they be much less contemptuous of the system which made their position of privilege possible. Professors were not always well paid. Second, that they soften their views of people who think differently. A little insight (one of the world's rarest commodities) is required to understand the needs and aspirations of the "other half."

I make no apology for returning once again to the hopes and aspirations of my constituents. Their views and the views of the educational and scientific estate are worlds apart. They need, or at least want, better housing, public and private transportation, better clothing, adequate money for recreation and entertainment. They might even aspire to own a colour television set. They do not belong to any of the privileged classes. In contrast to the academics, and many public officials as well, they think differently and they have a different set of personal and public priorities.

The preoccupation with the evils of industrialism is not new. It has exercised the minds of reformers for generations. It is not easy, nor always popular, to take a balanced view. Yet it is apparent that each new development is a mixed blessing. For every new benefit, there is an offsetting, though not always equal, disadvantage. It is a function of change and, perhaps, of life itself. Amelioration is possible but not without cost. The utopian world without flies and toads is just that – utopian, "nowhere."

Another of the partial truths that Galbraith has discovered is that the consumer has just recently lost control. "This means, obviously, that wants no longer originate with the consumer but with the producer."[3] I do not deny the fact. What I do deny is its novelty. Has it not always been the traders, transporters, scientists, investors, entrepreneurs and industrialists who have, by their actions, forced decisions from the rest of us? Our response may vary somewhat with affluence. But is the principle new? People have always been "led" to want things.

I have asked a number of old people if they could remember the introduction of electricity and electric lights as a substitute for candles. Had the candles bothered their eyes? Of course they had, although they were scarcely aware of it. Had they demanded a safer, better product, such as electricity? It had never occurred to them that such a thing was possible. The initiative began elsewhere. The consumer only entered the picture when there was a product available. Meanwhile, the process of invention, discovery, development, investment and marketing was taking place and the poor consumers were innocent of the whole affair. It was not of their doing.

I asked the oldest of my friends if he could recall the transition from horsedrawn to horseless carriages. Had this occurred in response to popular demand? Well hardly! It was just some restless, curious and inventive types tinkering away in the shop, trying to prove a point. Once proven, the developers, investors and salesmen had taken over. There had been no public outcry for a machine that would allow ordinary people to travel in style and at considerable speed. The whole thing had been thrust on them by those impossible types who insist on doing new things either for the profit involved or for the satisfaction gained from being part of the process, or both.

You cannot buy what you do not know about, but is any addition to the range of choice automatically bad? During my childhood, I had no notion that there was such a thing as an avocado. I was not exposed to them until I went to California in 1940. I did not really learn to like them until more recently when the supermarkets insisted on bringing them from the Pacific Coast and displaying them attractively to tempt me. Now I am hooked – and to my considerable enjoyment.

The same applies to other foods and products of the sea. I suppose I could have been perfectly happy without them, as other generations were, but some of them are so good that they really do add something to life's small pleasures.

But, you say, these are all natural products, they are not contrived. What about the most monstrous intrusion of all into our private lives, the television, especially the new coloured version? It is a perfect example. Like many of my contemporaries, I have become quite selective in what I watch. I have rediscovered books and prefer them to most television shows. But occasionally, for variety, or to be with the other members of the family, I watch a football game or a hockey match, the Rose Bowl parade, the launching of Apollo Eleven, or the "live by satellite" report of Canada Day at EXPO 70. Do I resent the availability of "exhibit No. 1" of the diabolical power the industrial machine has used to manipulate me? No. On the contrary, I would not want to be without it.

The same goes for the jet. Noise and air pollution notwithstanding, can anyone measure the adventure and pure delight of the new worlds opened up to tens of thousands of people who would not have known them otherwise, except through books and movies. There is visible history in Athens, fun in Paris, moonlight in the Caribbean. The migration of pale frozen Canadians to the lands of the sun in January cannot be all bad. If it is, I plead guilty.

As I mentioned earlier, each of these developments brings some new disadvantage to weigh against its benefit. Hydroelectric power has meant the desecration of some of the most magnificent natural beauty. Muskoka Falls near Bracebridge, Ontario has been destroyed. The automobiles have been responsible for unbelievable pollution, and now traffic strangulation. Perhaps the avocadoes will make me fat. Colour television can be a radiation hazard and jet airplanes can drive people up the wall. Few developments are "all good", and few developments are "all bad." The great majority produce benefits but also produce new problems that each generation, in its turn, must address.

Not every purchase is a prize. The late P.T. Barnum was quoted as saying that there was a sucker born every minute. Persuading people to part with their wealth in exchange for something of questionable value is an old technique. Most old-timers can remember the opportunities available at the Fall and district fairs. Professional barkers, mostly from the big cities, held their near rapturous audiences spellbound with the big words and magical claims attributable to the health potions and therapeutic waters then in vogue. Nearly everyone knew that the healing powers, like the benefits from the coloured pills dispensed by the family doctor, were largely imaginary; but they bought them anyway. Being taken was a form of sport. Today it is practiced on a grander scale. It is a scale based on mass media, mass production and mass consumption by a larger population with much more disposable wealth. The scale is different but the principle is the same. Human nature has not changed that much.

In the old days, when a product was too bad, or when the side effects were too great, the locals would run the barker out of town. In our more sophisticated society, we can run the modern barkers out of the country. Products that are harmful can be banned. Misleading advertising can be penalized. Frivolous products can be taxed as luxuries. Prices can be increased by making advertising a "non-deductible" expense. If society becomes completely fed up, it can ban advertising altogether. There is a wide range of legislative tools available if we want to use them.

Although I believe in strict control of harmful products, I do not believe that you can prevent new developments or stop industry from building markets by one means or another. This is a worldwide process and it is increasingly difficult to isolate people in one part of the world from what is going on elsewhere. To try is a form of censorship that will not work.

It would appear more profitable for society to use the tremendous capability of the industrial system to meet its needs. Selectivity and a degree of applied intelligence would be required. Dr. Galbraith suggests that the industrial system ignores state services not directly related to the system's needs. He offers Public Health Clinics as an example of a neglected service. Health is not the beneficiary of industrial promotion. I think this is a poor example. If health were exclusively administered by "private enterprise," some industrial giant would likely develop a market for "unit clinics." It would be a profitable operation. But much health care is administered by the state. The state has not called for development proposals for "unit clinics" to be followed by substantial orders for the successful submission. It could and the response would be inevitable. Industry will develop a product whenever and wherever it can either develop an assured market of its own (private) or be the recipient of one guaranteed by the state. Industry would be willing and anxious to cooperate. That is its role. It will cater to markets either of its own creation (cars) or of someone else's (missiles). If the state through its elected representatives or its permanent bureaucracy, or both, elects to develop and build missiles rather than unit clinics or urban transportation systems, missiles will be built. If, on the other hand, national priorities shift to clinics and transportation systems, so will the energy, support and genius of the industrial system.

Priorities of governments and peoples change from time to time, if slowly. So, too, do those of individuals. I suspect that people's priorities change as a function of many variables, including age and affluence. Many people whom I know personally consume only a small fraction of their income because that is what they want to do. Many of them put an increasing emphasis on leisure and family life, but in almost every case these are people who have all the basic necessities of life and more, and who feel secure. Doubtlessly, others, when they have satisfied their basic needs and wants, will modify their value judgments and priorities. The range of their real options will increase. Occasionally it may be inverse snobbery. There is no "loss" in taking the bus to work if everyone knows you can afford a second car. Occasionally it is a growing appreciation of what is important in life, and acting on it.

In considering the system of check and balances that might improve the present allocation of resources, Dr. Galbraith suggests that the educational and scientific estate will have to assume greater responsibility for political action and leadership. Its influence will check the power of big business. Presumably, it will also diffuse the power of big government, the bureaucrats and the generals. I wish I could be *sure* that it will restore to individuals some of the power they have lost to big business, big unions and big governments. Members of the educational and scientific estate are often autocratic by nature. They have all the answers even if they are not thoroughly familiar with the problems. Far from being under-rated by professional politicians and the press because of their ineptitude in politics, they are usually over-rated. The press stand in awe of the intellectual. So do professional politicians. I doubt that this should be the case because often the intellectual is the slickest talker and the poorest performer. More precisely, some intellectuals have their feet solidly on the ground and others are lounging on Cloud Nine. A number of the more grievous flaws in our present policies can be traced directly to the loungers. A mixture fairly representing all groups in society is much more likely to reflect the hopes and aspirations of that society than is domination by any single group.

If I appear to be critical of Galbraith, I am. Like most of my peers, however, I am a critical admirer. He is a genuine intellectual in the sense that what he writes often breaks new ground. In addition to writing delightfully, he interests and stimulates the mind. He would be the first to encourage cautionary and contrary argument. And, not least of all, he is a superb politician.

Notes

1. John Kenneth Galbraith, *The Affluent Society*, (Boston: Houghton-Mifflin Co., 1959).
2. J.K. Galbraith, *The New Industrial State*, (Boston: Houghton-Mifflin Co., 1971), p. 344.
3. J.K. Galbraith, *Weekend Magazine*, March 21, 1970.

Chapter **22**

Liberalism

In this chapter I am not going to attempt a treatise on liberalism. That is beyond my capability. Moreover, having reread some of the classic treatments, I suspect there is little that can be added to the millions of words already in print. A book has to end somewhere, however, and I have decided to do a brief review of the main points discussed throughout and to add a few closing thoughts.

I have often considered it strange, when listening to political debates, to observe the degree of consensus about goals among persons representing different parts of the political spectrum. Everyone favours greater justice, improved equality of opportunity, the elimination of poverty and an enhanced quality of life for all. Yet the means proposed to achieve these ends often seem to be diametrically opposed. In an attempt to explain this apparently irrational phenomenon, I have come to the conclusion that political philosophy is determined, above all, by one's economic belief and understanding. This suggestion is a generality, but an interesting one. In deciding which path to choose in achieving our goals, we are guided by what we believe to be possible, which, in turn, is influenced as much or more by observation as by deduction.

This hypothesis may explain why a greater percentage of some groups in society tend to support a traditional "left" position than would be the case with other groups. Historians, theologians, journalists and educators, though far from homogeneous in their political and economic beliefs, provide more than their proportionate share of reformers who believe that the economic system operated by the western liberal democracies is beyond repair and should be replaced by partial or total socialism. This has been learned at school and has been reinforced by personal observation of cyclical unemployment, economic stagnation and inequality. The obvious is inadequate. The not so obvious should be given a try.

Persons from these groups and others who are exposed to a broader experience including business and industry often tend to move away from this position, sometimes a step or two, and sometimes completely. Economics becomes more compelling to them. The necessity to meet a payroll on which other people are dependent provides its own discipline. Governmental regulation may be viewed as necessary to protect the public interest; but, in some cases, it will be seen merely as bureaucratic interference resulting in higher costs and consequently higher prices to the consumer. Exposed to the economics of reality, people tend to think and talk in terms of improvement of the system rather than its abandonment in favour of another that has been tried and found wanting.

That equally well-motivated people can come to such diametrically opposed positions in respect to means of achieving common goals is not surprising if one goes back to first principles – the premises on which alternate philosophies are based. One group believes that the "capitalist" (private capital) system is hopelessly inadequate and, therefore, doomed to collapse under its own weight. So why not give it a little push? The other group believes that in spite of its obvious deficiencies, the private capital system can be modified and changed to the extent necessary to make it as good or better than any other system, either real or hypothetical. So why not try to improve it?

It is in this context that the economic and political history of the last two centuries must be reviewed. My purpose throughout has been to question the premise on which much modern political thought has been based and, having concluded that it was a false premise, to support categorically the other side of the argument.

In reading the relevant history of the last two centuries, I discovered a collateral proposition. Simply stated, it is that most policy is re-active. Almost inevitably, institutional change follows technological change by decades or more. Problems are allowed to develop until they reach crisis or near-crisis proportions. Action is demanded. Solutions hastily conceived are often the wrong solutions but once adopted and put into practice, they are difficult to change. It is as if they had been set in concrete. Once copied by other nations and other cultures, the accepted wisdom is seldom challenged – successfully.

The evolution of economic systems is a classic example. The use of steam power and the specialization of labour revolutionized the process of production. Reform of the mechanics of distribution lagged by decades. It never has been contemporary. The consequences of this lag have been great and sometimes disastrous. The business cycles with their inevitable full employment and high unemployment peaks have caused unbelievable hardship and uncertainty. Humanitarians, horrified by the distress in human terms, reacted in the only way they knew. They rejected the system as fundamentally unacceptable and sought a genuine alternative. This approach neglected the possible correction of faults, which seemed elusive, and turned to the search of a new Utopia.

The answer, they thought, was socialism and so the giant ideological struggle began in earnest. Approaches differed from Fabianism to revolution, but the ends were the same in each case – a society where private wealth would no longer prevent justice to the masses and where each would contribute according to his ability and receive in accordance with his needs. The great ideal got its debut centre stage following the Bolshevik revolution. Notwithstanding a dash of pragmatism from time to time to provide flexibility, however, it failed in its objectives. Private wealth was eliminated but poverty and distress remained. The weaknesses in human nature were once again confirmed. Without the incentive attached to reasonable self interest, the economy performed in a lacklustre way. This was particularly true in agriculture where the connection between effort and reward is easy to observe and the independent spirit of enterprise impossible to erase. The system was found wanting.

All sorts of excuses have been offered but the principles cannot be ignored. Too much centralization of decision-making results in slow and poor decisions. Wealth and privilege, instead of being concentrated in the hands of capitalists, became the perquisites of government officials and party members. Officials treated the accumulated capital of the state as their own private preserve. The resultant "monopoly" demonstrates all the administrative and humanitarian weakness of giant size. People are treated as pawns and "property" of the state. The absolutism of ideas follows. The ideal of liberating man thus culminates in the most comprehensive repression and control.

The open system has been altered considerably, especially since World War II. An attempt has been made to maintain adequate aggregate demand and this has worked quite well on the whole, although some countries, like Japan, have achieved pre-eminent success. More recently, the rate of price inflation has risen to levels that are considered socially unacceptable in some countries. This phenomenon is due to the wage-price spiral and, on close examination, is easily explained. Nevertheless, Canada and the United States in particular, have decided to fight the traditional inflation of too much money chasing too few goods – a type of inflation that does not exist at the present time. This re-active policy – totally irrational – is history repeating itself. A temporary reduction in the rate of price increases in Canada has been achieved through a combination of lower profits, softer demand and a temporary price war amongst the food distributing supermarkets. Meanwhile, the growth rate on a per person basis has been reduced to near zero, unemployment has increased to intolerable levels, and the seeds of an even higher future price inflation have been sown. Wage and price controls in the rigid sector of the economy are essential and this can be done with the consistent application of traditional liberal principles.

Notwithstanding this temporary aberration, the liberal democratic approach offers advantages over all other systems.

If the necessary institutional changes are implemented, it will be possible to enjoy the most productive system from an economic standpoint, while maintaining the climate of freedom that allows the widest range of choice for individuals and groups within society. Full employment without inflation is a realizable goal. A fair and equitable – as distinct from equal – distribution of income can be achieved. Individuals and society can have a choice in the trade-off between production and leisure. More people will be given the opportunity to "do their own thing."

The invitation to do one's own thing may be interpreted as an appeal to self-interest. John Stuart Mill described freedom in this context. "The only freedom," he said, "which deserves the name is that of pursuing our own good, in our own way, so long as we do not attempt to deprive others of theirs, or impede their efforts to obtain it." My niece, when I read her this statement, remarked: "It's not very Christian, is it?" From the standpoint of personal morality, I find myself in agreement. One must add a version of the Golden Rule – do unto others as you would have them do unto you – to round it out. But Mill was a utilitarian and his rule is a most useful yardstick against which public policy can be measured in a pluralistic society. This kind of society does not prevent "loving thy neighbour as thyself" for those people who have the ability and inclination to observe that ideal.

Mill's suggestion of pursuing one's best interests within the limits imposed by respect for other people's freedom is coupled to the belief that this will produce the greatest good for the greatest numbers. The total range of activity and experience will be greater both quantitatively and qualitatively by large numbers of people pursuing, in the main, what they believe to be their own self-interest as opposed to someone else's self-interest – particularly if that someone else is as remote and impersonal as "the state."

It seems reasonable to suggest, then, that subject to proper safeguards the pursuit of self-interest is not entirely a bad thing. This was the conclusion of John Maynard Keynes who wrote this testimony:

Let us stop for a moment to remind ourselves what these advantages are. They are partly advantages of efficiency – the advantages of decentralisation and of the play of self-interest. The advantage to efficiency of the decentralisation of decisions and of individual responsibility is even greater, perhaps, than the nineteenth century supposed; and the reaction against the appeal to self-interest may have gone too far. But above all, individualism, if it can be purged of its defects and its abuses, is the best safeguard of personal liberty in the sense that, compared with any other system, it greatly widens the field for the exercise of personal choice. It is also the best safeguard of the variety of life, which emerges precisely from this extended field of personal choice, and the loss of which is the greatest of all the losses of the homogeneous or totalitarian state. For this variety preserves the traditions which embody the most secure and successful choices of former generations; it colours the present with the diversification of its fancy; and, being the handmaid of experiment as well as of tradition and of fancy, it is the most powerful instrument to better the future.[1]

Although I am willing to accept both the efficiency and the usefulness of the utilitarian approach in a pluralistic society, I must insist that the definition of "utility" be sufficiently broad as to include those things that contribute to the spiritual good of man but that are not always included in the "goods" of the economist. Man does not live by bread alone. As basic needs of food, clothing and shelter are met, men turn more and more to the "quality of life" options. These include clean fresh air, clean water and unspoiled open spaces where one can enjoy the variety of nature. Whether it is the beauty of the setting sun or the wonder of millions of icy diamonds on a winter day, there is a majesty in nature which stirs the dullest soul. Even the most gregarious of men have need of the physical and spiritual refurbishment of solitude. Mill described this need beautifully in his *Principles*:

It is not good for man to be kept perforce at all times in the presence of his species. A world from which solitude is extirpated is a very poor ideal. Solitude, in the sense of being often alone, is essential to any depth of meditation or of character; and solitude in the presence of natural beauty and grandeur, is the cradle of thoughts and aspirations which are not only good for the individual, but which society could ill do without. Nor is there much satisfaction in contemplating the world with nothing left to the spontaneous activity of nature; with every rood of land brought into cultivation, which is capable of growing food for human beings; every flowery waste or natural pasture ploughed up, all quadrupeds or birds which are not domesticated for man's use exterminated as his rivals for food, every hedgerow or superfluous tree rooted out, and scarcely a place left where a wild shrub or flower could grow without being eradicated as a weed in the name of improved agriculture. If the earth must lose that great portion of its pleasantness which it owes to things that the unlimited increase of wealth and population would extirpate from it, for the mere purpose of enabling it to support a larger, but not a better or a happier population, I sincerely hope, for the sake of posterity, that they will be content to be stationary, long before necessity compels them to it.[2]

When access to nature's beauty, variety of experience and other quality of life standards are included with "things," the line between utilitarian and humanitarian becomes indistinct. One is the handmaid of the other. Any system that produces the maximum product for the least effort, particularly in respect of work that is boring and a drudge, must be the most humane. The system that provides the widest range of choice to individuals and groups, thereby providing the maximum in "tailor made" circumstances and experiences must be the most humane. Individuals must be treated as people and not as ants. Personal consideration, which tends to be lost as the state becomes the "end" rather than the "means," must surely be the essence of human existence. People must be loved, cared for and needed as individuals as well as members of a large group. The system that encourages the most individual attention based on individual initiative and concern must be, by definition, the most humane.

In addition to its potential for people as individuals, the open system – the liberal democratic option – provides the best system of checks and balances. In a state where most or all of the capital is administered by the state, the range of choice is limited. No competing network or publisher is available to hire a commentator or columnist who has incurred the disfavour of the establishment. Inventions turned down by the authorities as impractical or premature cannot be taken to competitive entrepreneurs or developers. Politicians who differ with the party will be obliged to seek "employment" in another field if, in fact, they have their freedom to do so. In a liberal democratic society, the practical range of choice may be limited but there are options.

Within the liberal democratic society, the true liberal will want to limit any concentration of power as much as practicable. This has been a traditional role of liberalism. It does not matter whether the villain is a powerful church, business cartel, labour union or government.

When a concentration of power becomes so great that it is used detrimentally to the public interest, it has to be curtailed. When a central government occupies fields of authority that could better be exercised at the state or local level, a reassessment should occur. When a state government occupies a field that could be better administered at the municipal level, a realignment should take place. When any level of government takes power from the people for the purpose of making decisions which could be more appropriately made by individuals themselves, a reversal is called for. The rule should be the maximum decentralization of authority and decision-making consistent with the effective pursuit of agreed goals and objectives. Alienation is a function of both size and distance. Big government and remote government are both major contributors.

Big business must be subject to the same philosophy. Competition should be encouraged where competition is a reasonable policy and likely to be effective. In some cases, due to the size and complexity of the operation, competition is not possible. Then, guidelines to protect the public interest are required.

Big labour, too, must not be permitted to exercise power contrary to the public interest. No group should be allowed to blackmail the public at large by failing to deliver the electric power, the mails or the food on which an interdependent society relies. Nor should anyone be allowed to leave the garbage uncollected, the sewage untreated or the sick unattended. We are too interdependent for that. We have to rely on each other – each to do his duty.

At the same time, we have to recognize who our real heroes are. The boy who delivers my newspapers at the crack of dawn, fair weather or foul, is one of my heroes. The postman who brings me many little surprises, including bills, but letters too, some kind and some insulting, is another. The garbage man is a favourite. I really rely on him. I do not really know what he does with the stuff but I am grateful that he takes it away. The mechanics who service the airplanes I fly in get special mention. They literally hold my life in their hands and I am constantly grateful to them for their painstaking and meticulous care.

Heroes have to be treated fairly, and if they are, if they are given a fair share of the nation's increased production along with other groups in society and if, once having got it, the extra money will buy something extra, they will not want to strike. They cannot afford the luxury of strikes anymore than their neighbours can.

The freedom to have your basic services performed, without interruption, it seems to me, must join the right to work and the right to receive a fair return for that work as additions to the basic freedoms already well established. Perhaps these fundamental economic rights will be just as difficult to establish as freedom of speech, freedom of assembly, freedom of the press, freedom of religion and freedom from arbitrary arrest were in their time. But fundamental they are and accepted they must be. Interdependence must be recognized and kept from arbitrary disruption.

Having stated these freedoms as basic and unalterable and having enshrined them in our laws or in our customs, we still must protect them from encroachment by constant vigilance. Nearly all constitutions provide for the abrogation of civil rights in time of national emergency. Amongst provisions for a patriated Canadian Constitution released at the end of the Third Working Session of the Constitutional Conference, one reads the following:

> *The exercise of these freedoms may be subject only to such limitations as are prescribed by law and as are reasonably justifiable in a democratic society in the interests of national security, public safety, health or morals or the fundamental rights and freedoms of others.*[3]

This caveat is sufficiently broad that it could be the basis, in time of real or apprehended crisis, of near total negation of civil rights and fundamental freedoms by any government that was so inclined.

In the final analysis, the use or abuse of any extraordinary powers will depend on the quality of the people themselves. The general level of understanding of fundamental rights and freedoms and the degree of conviction with which they are held will determine the zeal with which they are upheld. It is people and their individual convictions forming a consensus which will prevail.

The same considerations will apply in respect of the operation of the political system at large. So much will depend on the quality of the people as individuals. In my tour of the Pacific in 1970, I sensed, instinctively, that economic progress in its many manifestations was a function not just of those factors that are usually discussed by economists but also of the incorruptibility of the people and their public men. It might be a difficult thesis to prove – but I believe it on the basis of my own observations.

I have put the emphasis on individual conviction, individual morality and integrity because I believe that is cardinal to a successful and happy society. I have rejected the notion of a morality imposed by the state. It smacks of authoritarianism. Morality cannot be legislated, but it can be taught. Our awareness of our responsibility to others, our government's awareness of its responsibility to meet people's needs, our relationship with other nations will be influenced by a collective morality – or lack of it – which can be nothing more than the sum of individual morality.

Perhaps this is why, as an individual, I have rejected Marxism and its several variations. Although designed to help and emancipate ordinary people, its practical implementation has involved revolution and bloodshed. Later disciples continue in the same vein, speaking of world revolution. Mao-Tse-Tung tells us, in essence, that good Marxist believers will love their friends and hate their enemies. The only power worthy of the name is the power that comes from the barrel of a gun.

Surely this approach is less than civilized. The suffering and misery resulting from revolution is always as bad or worse than the disease it attempts to cure. Is it axiomatic that a good end justifies bad means even when revolution and war or civil war is involved? I cannot think so. Surely there is a more intelligent humane method of achieving change. In theory, at least, insensitivity to the people's needs can be censured at the polls.

The alternative is too absolute. Blind obedience to

ideology and its tactics robs the ideologists of their humanity. Toronto *Globe and Mail* correspondent Norman Webster reported from Peking that the lending of reactionary novels to poison young minds was considered a blatant and dangerous debasement. How tenuous is the Marxist ideal that it can tolerate no competition?

A press release from Katmandu in April 1970 reported that Tibetan Lamas were being forced by Chinese Communists to read revolutionary literature rather than their own prayer books. Those who refused were reportedly either killed or publicly abused, their "bodies . . . dragged along the streets while Tibetans were forced to line up along the route and spit and throw dust at them."

Is that the kind of emancipation of human life that young people are seeking? Is that the kind of peace they have in mind when the well-known finger sign is raised idealistically? I doubt it. This is a travesty of justice; it is a travesty of humanitarianism; it is a travesty of civilization; it is a travesty of peace and all in the name of a kind of materialism that is not too different from the one abhored.

One recalls Aristotle's saying, "man when separated from law and justice is the worst of all animals." This judgment has stood the test of history. Several times civilizations have developed constitutional government and moved away from barbarism toward a civilized existence. In each case, eventually, there has been a breakdown in the rule of law in favour of violence and anarchy.

In a 1970 article the London Observer eloquently summarizes the lesson of our moral and social history.

> *It has taught us that, though progress may be cumulative in the fields of science and technology, there is no such thing as cumulative progress toward an ever greater humanity in our treatment of each other. In the social and spiritual fields, the battle for humanity . . . has to be fought by every human being in his own soul.*

This is the unanimous teaching of all the historic religions and philosophies.

At this point I would like to proclaim that I am not as pessimistic about the future of the world as some of my contemporaries are. The world has suffered a continual series of wars, insurrections, famines, plagues and floods and each time has managed to survive. Often, too, some small legacy of good manages to emerge from the ashes. It is unrealistic to expect the patterns of human nature and history to alter abruptly or permanently. But the struggle for improvement must go on and each generation must be made aware of the exciting challenge on its doorstep if only the available tools are humanely and intelligently applied.

It is my awareness of the cyclic success in man's constant struggle with good and evil that has led me to speak in terms of an improved system and a liberal approach which will be as immune as possible to the ebb and flow of social and moral evolution. I do not believe that mass Utopia is a realizable goal. I firmly believe that dramatic and substantial improvement is a real possibility. The higher the standard of collective morality and concern, at any time, the higher the real potential.

The best results also depend on a recognition of the dynamics of change. Not change for its own sake but change compelled by a changing environment. Technology will not observe the status quo. It moves and with its movement the ground rules change as to what is possible. Institutions must quickly adjust because the abstract perfection of yesterday is merely an outmoded conservatism today.

A dynamic liberalism is the best vehicle for orderly change. The late and great Canadian journalist, John W. Dafoe said of liberalism:

(It) is on one side of the playing field and all the other isms from Toryism to Communism on the other side. The division is between the libertarian and the authoritarian concept of life; between the view that the state is the agency created by the collective action of individuals to do those things for themselves which it is expedient and desirable to do collectively, and the other view that the state is leviathan and that the souls and lives of men are disposable by it.

I believe that rational change can best take place in a decentralized society where man, not the State, is supreme. Rational change will permit us to keep our basic freedoms, and to add those new ones necessary to enhance our quality of life. Full employment and stable prices will give us the maximum range of choice with which to assert equality of opportunity and justice for all. This is the liberalism I espouse. It is not a liberalism of the left or of the right but, I believe, a rational and, above all, humane liberalism.

Notes

1. John M. Keynes, *The General Theory of Employment, Interest, and Money,* (London: 1960), Macmillan & Co. Ltd. and Harcourt, Brace & Jovanovich, p. 380.
2. Reprinted from Book IV, chapter vi of *Principles of Political Economy* by John Stuart Mill, text edited by J.M. Robson (*Collected Works of John Stuart Mill,* General Editor: F.E.L. Priestley), by permission of University of Toronto Press and Routledge and Kegan Paul. © University of Toronto Press 1965.
3. Statement of Conclusion, p. 4, The Third Working Session of the Constitutional Conference, February 8-9, 1971, in Ottawa.